Literature From Around the World

PRENTICE HALL
Upper Saddle River, New Jersey
Needham, Massachusetts

ISBN 0-13-435451-6

5 6 7 8 9 10   02 01 00 99

PRENTICE HALL

Acknowledgments

Grateful acknowledgment is made to the following for copyrighted material:

American University in Cairo Press

"Half a Day" as "Nisf yowm" short story by Naguib Mahfouz from *al-Fagr al-kadhib* (The False Dawn). Copyright © 1991 by the American University in Cairo Press. Reprinted by permission of the publisher.

Doubleday, a division of Bantam Doubleday Dell Publishing Group, Inc. and Harold Ober Associates, Inc.

"Marriage is a Private Affair" from *Girls at War and Other Stories* by Chinua Achebe. Copyright © 1972, 1973 by Chinua Achebe. Used by permission of Doubleday, a division of Bantam Doubleday Dell Publishing Group, Inc. and Harold Ober Associates, Inc.

Farrar, Straus & Giroux, Inc.

"Sunday Lemons" from *Collected Poems 1948–1984* by Derek Walcott. Copyright © 1986 by Derek Walcott. "What I Have Been Doing Lately" from *At the Bottom of the River*, by Jamaica Kincaid. Copyright 1983 by Jamaica Kincaid. Reprinted by permission of Farrar, Straus & Giroux, Inc.

Foreign Languages Press, Beijing

Excerpt from *From Emperor to Citizen: The Autobiography of Aisin-Gioro P'u Yi*. Copyright © 1964, 1965 by Foreign Languages Press. Copyright © 1987 by Oxford University Press. Reprinted by permission of Foreign Languages Press, Beijing.

(Acknowledgments continue on p. 162.)

Contents

Introduction

Writings from twentieth-century authors explore a vast range of issues—from the horrors of war to the absurdities of everyday existence. Although the writers in this anthology come from different continents, countries, and towns, they explore experiences and themes that transcend time and place.

Europe in the first half of the twentieth century was an arena of war, in which the Great War, the Russian Revolution, and World War II largely took place. You can trace the events as well as the mood of the times through literature such as Elie Wiesel's documentation of the real-life horrors of being imprisoned in a German concentration camp and Albert Camus's fictional tale set in war-torn Algeria. Although the countries of Europe are small and distances between them slight, their citizens celebrate and revere their distinct cultural heritages. For example, in fictional works by writers James Joyce, Stanislaw Lem, and Isak Dinesen, their individual cultural identities clearly emerge.

Asia in the twentieth century became an interesting mix of old and new. Some Asian nations saw rapid change as they became world leaders in the manufacture of technological products and automobiles. But within those same nations and throughout many smaller countries, the twentieth century left rural villages and towns virtually untouched. The effects and after-effects of colonialism, too, had a lasting impact on the lives of many Asians.

In Santha Rama Rau's essay "By Any Other Name," for example, the author shows how racist attitudes of the British toward Indians during the colonial years had a profound impact on her life. Japanese cultural behavior undergoes scrutiny in Yukio Mishima's "The Pearl" and Akutagawa Ryunosuke's "The Nose." And Aisin-Gioro P'u Yi, the last emperor of China, shares with the world what it was like to grow up as the emperor in the Forbidden City.

Many nations of Africa, too, have been greatly affected by colonialization and decolonialization by European countries, natural disasters like floods and famine, and civil wars and cruel dictatorships. Apartheid, a racially discriminatory economic system, was finally abolished in South Africa, and blacks won a voice in government. These issues have been the focus of several African writers. For example, racial discrimination is addressed by Wole Soyinka and Mark Mathabane in "Telephone Conversation" and *Kaffir Boy*, and Chinua Achebe's "Marriage Is a Private Affair" is a riveting story of how changing cultural attitudes rip a family apart.

The Middle East has been the focus of world attention throughout much of the twentieth century. Following the Holocaust of

World War II, a part of Palestine was designated the new homeland for Jews; however, many Arab nations refused to recognize
the legitimacy of the new country of Israel, and the area has
been plagued by war and terrorism ever since. Yehuda Amichai's
poem "Lament for the War Dead" was written following a bomb-
ing attack on Israel the night of Yom Kippur. Egypt's Naguib
Mahfouz's short story "Half a Day," which comments on the
rapid modernization of the ancient city of Cairo, may also sug-
gest that a modern, global attitude may soon replace a narrow,
nationalistic one.

Dictatorships, guerrilla warfare, political scandals, and revolu-
tions have rocked the Americas in the twentieth century. The
writers of these diverse nations express their ideas vividly and
memorably, often using elements of fantasy within their literary
works. Using the backdrop of World War II, Borges's "The Garden
of Forking Paths" is a spy thriller that revolves around a fantastic puzzle. In "Axolotl," Julio Cortazar takes fantasy a step further as the narrator transforms into a fish. Jamaica Kincaid, too,
weaves fantasy through words in "What I Have Been Doing
Lately," and Derek Walcott explores dimensions of meaning in a
poem about a bowl of lemons.

Our world is a truly remarkable place, inhabited by extraordinary people. As you read each selection in this collection, allow
yourself to be transported to the time and place created by each
author. Then celebrate the differences among cultures even as
you recognize and respond to the common elements that bind
humanity together.

The Enchanted Garden

Italo Calvino

Translated by Archibald Colquhoun and Peggy Wright

GIOVANNINO and Serenella were strolling along the railroad tracks. Below was a scaly sea of somber, clear blue; above, a sky lightly streaked with white clouds. The railroad tracks were shimmering and burning hot. It was fun going along the tracks, there were so many games to play—he balancing on one rail and holding her hand while she walked along on the other, or else both jumping from one sleeper to the next without ever letting their feet touch the stones in between. Giovannino and Serenella had been out looking for crabs, and now they had decided to explore the railroad tracks as far as the tunnel. He liked playing with Serenella, for she did not behave as all the other little girls did, forever getting frightened or bursting into tears at every joke. Whenever Giovannino said, "Let's go there," or "Let's do this," Serenella followed without a word.

Ping! They both gave a start and looked up. A telephone wire had snapped off the top of the pole. It sounded like an iron stork shutting its beak in a hurry. They stood with their noses in the air and watched. What a pity not to have seen it! Now it would never happen again.

"There's a train coming," said Giovannino.

Serenella did not move from the rail. "Where from?" she asked.

Giovannino looked around in a knowledgeable way. He pointed at the black hole of the tunnel, which showed clear one moment, then misty the next, through the invisible heat haze rising from the stony track.

"From there," he said. It was as though they already heard a snort from the darkness of the tunnel, and saw the train suddenly appear, belching out fire and smoke, the wheels mercilessly eating up the rails as it hurtled toward them.

"Where shall we go, Giovannino?"

There were big gray aloes down by the sea, surrounded by dense, impenetrable nettles, while up the hillside ran a rambling hedge with thick leaves but no flowers. There was still no sign of the train; perhaps it was coasting, with the engine cut off, and would jump out at them all of a sudden. But Giovannino had

now found an opening in the hedge. "This way," he called.

The fence under the rambling hedge was an old bent rail. At one point it twisted about on the ground like the corner of a sheet of paper. Giovannino had slipped into the hole and already half vanished.

"Give me a hand, Giovannino."

They found themselves in the corner of a garden, on all fours in a flower bed, with their hair full of dry leaves and moss. Everything was quiet; not a leaf was stirring.

"Come on," said Giovannino, and Serenella nodded in reply.

There were big old flesh-colored eucalyptus trees and winding gravel paths. Giovannino and Serenella tiptoed along the paths, taking care not to crunch the gravel. Suppose the owners appeared now?

Everything was so beautiful: sharp bends in the path and high, curling eucalyptus leaves and patches of sky. But there was always the worrying thought that it was not their garden, and that they might be chased away any moment. Yet not a sound could be heard. A flight of chattering sparrows rose from a clump of arbutus at a turn in the path. Then all was silent again. Perhaps it was an abandoned garden?

But the shade of the big trees came to an end, and they found themselves under the open sky facing flower beds filled with neat rows of petunias and convolvulus, and paths and balustrades and rows of box trees. And up at the end of the garden was a large villa with flashing windowpanes and yellow-and-orange curtains.

And it was all quite deserted. The two children crept forward, treading carefully over the gravel: perhaps the windows would suddenly be flung open, and angry ladies and gentlemen appear on the terraces to unleash great dogs down the paths. Now they found a wheelbarrow standing near a ditch. Giovannino picked it up by the handles and began pushing it along: it creaked like a whistle at every turn. Serenella seated herself in it and they moved slowly forward, Giovannino pushing the barrow with her on top, along the flower beds and fountains.

Every now and then Serenella would point to a flower and say in a low voice, "That one," and Giovannino would put the barrow down, pluck it, and give it to her. Soon she had a lovely bouquet.

Eventually the gravel ended and they reached an open space paved in bricks and mortar. In the middle of this space was a big empty rectangle: a swimming pool. They crept up to the edge;

it was lined with blue tiles and filled to the brim with clear water. How lovely it would be to swim in!

"Shall we go for a dip?" Giovannino asked Serenella. The idea must have been quite dangerous if he asked her instead of just saying, "In we go!" But the water was so clear and blue, and Serenella was never afraid. She jumped off the barrow and put her bunch of flowers in it. They were already in bathing suits, since they'd been out for crabs before. Giovannino plunged in—not from the diving board, because the splash would have made too much noise, but from the edge of the pool. Down and down he went with his eyes wide open, seeing only the blue from the tiles and his pink hands like goldfish; it was not the same as under the sea, full of shapeless green-black shadows. A pink form appeared above him: Serenella! He took her hand and they swam up to the surface, a bit anxiously. No, there was no one watching them at all. But it was not so nice as they'd thought it would be; they always had that uncomfortable feeling that they had no right to any of this, and might be chased out at any moment.

They scrambled out of the water, and there beside the swimming pool they found a Ping-Pong table. Instantly Giovannino picked up the paddle and hit the ball, and Serenella, on the other side, was quick to return his shot. And so they went on playing, though giving only light taps at the ball, in case someone in the villa heard them. Then Giovannino, in trying to parry a shot that had bounced high, sent the ball sailing away through the air and smack against a gong hanging in a pergola. There was a long, somber boom. The two children crouched down behind a clump of ranunculus. At once two menservants in white coats appeared, carrying big trays; when they had put the trays down on a round table under an orange-and-yellow-striped umbrella, off they went.

Giovannino and Serenella crept up to the table. There was tea, milk, and sponge cake. They had only to sit down and help themselves. They poured out two cups of tea and cut two slices of cake. But somehow they did not feel at all at ease, and sat perched on the edge of their chairs, their knees shaking. And they could not really enjoy the tea and cake, for nothing seemed to have any taste. Everything in the garden was like that: lovely but impossible to enjoy properly, with that worrying feeling inside that they were only there through an odd stroke of luck, and the fear that they'd soon have to give an account of themselves.

Very quietly they tiptoed up to the villa. Between the slits of a Venetian blind they saw a beautiful shady room, with collections

of butterflies hanging on the walls. And in the room was a pale little boy. Lucky boy, he must be the owner of this villa and garden.
He was stretched out on a chaise lounge, turning the pages of a
large book filled with figures. He had big white hands and wore
pajamas buttoned up to the neck, though it was summer.

As the two children went on peeping through the slits, the
pounding of their hearts gradually subsided. Why, the little rich
boy seemed to be sitting there and turning the pages and glanc-
ing around with more anxiety and worry than their own. Then
he got up and tiptoed around, as if he were afraid that at any
moment someone would come and turn him out, as if he felt
that that book, that chaise lounge, and those butterflies framed
on the wall, the garden and games and tea trays, the swimming
pool and paths, were only granted to him by some enormous
mistake, as if he were incapable of enjoying them and felt the
bitterness of the mistake as his own fault.

The pale boy was wandering about his shady room furtively,
touching with his white fingers the edges of the cases studded
with butterflies; then he stopped to listen. The pounding of Giovannino and Serenella's hearts, which had died down, now got
harder than ever. Perhaps it was the fear of a spell that hung
over this villa and garden and over all these lovely, comfortable
things, the residue of some injustice committed long ago.

Clouds darkened the sun. Very quietly Giovannino and Serenella crept away. They went back along the same paths they had
come, stepping fast but never at a run. And they went through
the hedge again on all fours. Between the aloes they found a path
leading down to the small, stony beach, with banks of seaweed
along the shore. Then they invented a wonderful new game: a
seaweed fight. They threw great handfuls of it in each other's
faces till late in the afternoon. And Serenella never once cried.

The Joy of Writing

Wisława Szymborska

Why does this written doe bound through these written woods?
For a drink of written water from a spring
whose surface will xerox her soft muzzle?
Why does she lift her head; does she hear something?
Perched on four slim legs borrowed from the truth,
she pricks up her ears beneath my fingertips.
Silence—this word also rustles across the page
and parts the boughs
that have sprouted from the word "woods."

Lying in wait, set to pounce on the blank page,
are letters up to no good,
clutches of clauses so subordinate
they'll never let her get away.

Each drop of ink contains a fair supply
of hunters, equipped with squinting eyes behind their sights,
prepared to swarm the sloping pen at any moment,
surround the doe, and slowly aim their guns.

They forget that what's here isn't life.
Other laws, black on white, obtain.
The twinkling of an eye will take as long as I say,
and will, if I wish, divide into tiny eternities,
full of bullets stopped in mid-flight.
Not a thing will ever happen unless I say so.
Without my blessing, not a leaf will fall,
not a blade of grass will bend beneath that little hoof's full stop.

Is there then a world
where I rule absolutely on fate?
A time I bind with chains of signs?
An existence become endless at my bidding?

The joy of writing.
The power of preserving.
Revenge of a mortal hand.

from
Night

Elie Wiesel

Translated by Stella Rodway

Following is an excerpt from Night, a nonfiction account of Elie Wiesel's imprisonment by the Nazis during World War II. The narrative begins soon after Elie and his family are taken prisoner by Nazis and sent by train to an unknown destination.

THE train stopped at Kaschau, a little town on the Czechoslovak frontier. We realized then that we were not going to stay in Hungary. Our eyes were opened, but too late.

The door of the car slid open. A German officer, accompanied by a Hungarian lieutenant-interpreter, came up and introduced himself.

"From this moment, you come under the authority of the German army. Those of you who still have gold, silver, or watches in your possession must give them up now. Anyone who is later found to have kept anything will be shot on the spot. Secondly, anyone who feels ill may go to the hospital car. That's all."

The Hungarian lieutenant went among us with a basket and collected the last possessions from those who no longer wished to taste the bitterness of terror.

"There are eighty of you in this wagon," added the German officer. "If anyone is missing, you'll all be shot, like dogs. . . ."

They disappeared. The doors were closed. We were caught in a trap, right up to our necks. The doors were nailed up; the way back was finally cut off. The world was a cattle wagon hermetically sealed.

We had a woman with us named Madame Schächter. She was about fifty; her ten-year-old son was with her, crouched in a corner. Her husband and two eldest sons had been deported with the first transport by mistake. The separation had completely broken her.

I knew her well. A quiet woman with tense, burning eyes, she had often been to our house. Her husband, who was a pious man, spent his days and nights in study, and it was she who worked to support the family.

Madame Schächter had gone out of her mind. On the first day of the journey she had already begun to moan and to keep asking why she had been separated from her family. As time went on, her cries grew hysterical.

On the third night, while we slept, some of us sitting one against the other and some standing, a piercing cry split the silence:

"Fire! I can see a fire! I can see a fire!"

There was a moment's panic. Who was it who had cried out? It was Madame Schächter. Standing in the middle of the wagon, in the pale light from the windows, she looked like a withered tree in a cornfield. She pointed her arm toward the window, screaming:

"Look! Look at it! Fire! A terrible fire! Mercy! *Oh, that fire!*"

Some of the men pressed up against the bars. There was nothing there; only the darkness.

The shock of this terrible awakening stayed with us for a long time. We still trembled from it. With every groan of the wheels on the rail, we felt that an abyss was about to open beneath our bodies. Powerless to still our own anguish, we tried to console ourselves:

"She's mad, poor soul. . . ."

Someone had put a damp cloth on her brow, to calm her, but still her screams went on:

"Fire! Fire!"

Her little boy was crying, hanging onto her skirt, trying to take hold of her hands. "It's all right, Mummy! There's nothing there. . . . Sit down. . . ." This shook me even more than his mother's screams had done.

Some women tried to calm her. "You'll find your husband and your sons again . . . in a few days. . . ."

She continued to scream, breathless, her voice broken by sobs. "Jews, listen to me! I can see a fire! There are huge flames! It is a furnace!"

It was as though she were possessed by an evil spirit which spoke from the depths of her being.

We tried to explain it away, more to calm ourselves and to recover our own breath than to comfort her. "She must be very thirsty, poor thing! That's why she keeps talking about a fire devouring her."

But it was in vain. Our terror was about to burst the sides of the train. Our nerves were at breaking point. Our flesh was creeping. It was as though madness were taking possession of

us all. We could stand it no longer. Some of the young men forced her to sit down, tied her up, and put a gag in her mouth.

Silence again. The little boy sat down by his mother, crying. I had begun to breathe normally again. We could hear the wheels churning out that monotonous rhythm of a train traveling through the night. We could begin to doze, to rest, to dream. . . .

An hour or two went by like this. Then another scream took our breath away. The woman had broken loose from her bonds and was crying out more loudly than ever:

"Look at the fire! Flames, flames everywhere. . . ."

Once more the young men tied her up and gagged her. They even struck her. People encouraged them:

"Make her be quiet! She's mad! Shut her up! She's not the only one. She can keep her mouth shut. . . ."

They struck her several times on the head—blows that might have killed her. Her little boy clung to her; he did not cry out; he did not say a word. He was not even weeping now.

An endless night. Toward dawn, Madame Schächter calmed down. Crouched in her corner, her bewildered gaze scouring the emptiness, she could no longer see us.

She stayed like that all through the day, dumb, absent, isolated among us. As soon as night fell, she began to scream: "There's a fire over there!" She would point at a spot in space, always the same one. They were tired of hitting her. The heat, the thirst, the pestilential stench, the suffocating lack of air— these were as nothing compared with these screams which tore us to shreds. A few days more and we should all have started to scream, too.

But we had reached a station. Those who were next to the windows told us its name:

"Auschwitz."

No one had ever heard that name.

The train did not start up again. The afternoon passed slowly. Then the wagon doors slid open. Two men were allowed to get down to fetch water.

When they came back, they told us that, in exchange for a gold watch, they had discovered that this was the last stop. We would be getting out here. There was a labor camp. Conditions were good. Families would not be split up. Only the young people would go to work in the factories. The old men and invalids would be kept occupied in the fields.

The barometer of confidence soared. Here was a sudden re-

lease from the terrors of the previous nights. We gave thanks to God.

Madame Schächter stayed in her corner, wilted, dumb, indifferent to the general confidence. Her little boy stroked her hand.

As dusk fell, darkness gathered inside the wagon. We started to eat our last provisions. At ten in the evening, everyone was looking for a convenient position in which to sleep for a while, and soon we were all asleep. Suddenly:

"The fire! The furnace! Look, over there! . . ."

Waking with a start, we rushed to the window. Yet again we had believed her, even if only for a moment. But there was nothing outside save the darkness of night. With shame in our souls, we went back to our places, gnawed by fear, in spite of ourselves. As she continued to scream, they began to hit her again, and it was with the greatest difficulty that they silenced her.

The man in charge of our wagon called a German officer who was walking about on the platform, and asked him if Madame Schächter could be taken to the hospital car.

"You must be patient," the German replied. "She'll be taken there soon."

Toward eleven o'clock, the train began to move. We pressed against the windows. The convoy was moving slowly. A quarter of an hour later, it slowed down again. Through the windows we could see barbed wire; we realized that this must be the camp.

We had forgotten the existence of Madame Schächter. Suddenly, we heard terrible screams:

"Jews, look! Look through the window! Flames! Look!"

And as the train stopped, we saw this time that flames were gushing out of a tall chimney into the black sky.

Madame Schächter was silent herself. Once more she had become dumb, indifferent, absent, and had gone back to her corner.

We looked at the flames in the darkness. There was an abominable odor floating in the air. Suddenly, our doors opened. Some odd-looking characters, dressed in striped shirts and black trousers, leapt into the wagon. They held electric torches and truncheons. They began to strike out to right and left, shouting:

"Everybody get out! Everyone out of the wagon! Quickly!"

We jumped out. I threw a last glance toward Madame Schächter. Her little boy was holding her hand.

In front of us flames. In the air that smell of burning flesh. It must have been about midnight. We had arrived—at Birkenau,

reception center for Auschwitz.

The cherished objects we had brought with us thus far were left behind in the train, and with them, at last, our illusions.

Every two yards or so an SS man held his Tommy gun trained on us. Hand in hand we followed the crowd.

An SS noncommissioned officer came to meet us, a truncheon in his hand. He gave the order:

"Men to the left! Women to the right!"

Eight words spoken quietly, indifferently, without emotion. Eight short, simple words. Yet that was the moment when I parted from my mother. I had not had time to think, but already I felt the pressure of my father's hand: we were alone. For a part of a second I glimpsed my mother and my sisters moving away to the right. Tzipora held Mother's hand. I saw them disappear into the distance; my mother was stroking my sister's fair hair, as though to protect her, while I walked on with my father and the other men. And I did not know that in that place, at that moment, I was parting from my mother and Tzipora forever. I went on walking. My father held onto my hand.

Behind me, an old man fell to the ground. Near him was an SS man, putting his revolver back in its holster.

My hand shifted on my father's arm. I had one thought—not to lose him. Not to be left alone.

The SS officers gave the order:

"Form fives!"

Commotion. At all costs we must keep together.

"Here, kid, how old are you?"

It was one of the prisoners who asked me this. I could not see his face, but his voice was tense and weary.

"I'm not quite fifteen yet."

"No. Eighteen."

"But I'm not," I said, "Fifteen."

"Fool. Listen to what *I* say."

Then he questioned my father, who replied:

"Fifty."

The other grew more furious than ever.

"No, not fifty. Forty. Do you understand? Eighteen and forty."

He disappeared into the night shadows. A second man came up, spitting oaths at us.

"What have you come here for, you sons of bitches? What are you doing here, eh?"

Someone dared to answer him.

"What do you think? Do you suppose we've come here for our own pleasure? Do you think we asked to come?"

A little more, and the man would have killed him.

"You shut your trap, you filthy swine, or I'll squash you right now! You'd have done better to have hanged yourselves where you were than come here. Didn't you know what was in store for you at Auschwitz? Haven't you heard about it? In 1944?"

No, we had not heard. No one had told us. He could not believe his ears. His tone of voice became increasingly brutal.

"Do you see that chimney over there? See it? Do you see those flames? (Yes, we did see the flames.) Over there—that's where you're going to be taken. That's your grave, over there. Haven't you realized it yet? You dumb bastards, don't you understand anything? You're going to be burned. Frizzled away. Turned into ashes."

He was growing hysterical in his fury. We stayed motionless, petrified. Surely it was all a nightmare? An unimaginable nightmare?

I heard murmurs around me.

"We've got to do something. We can't let ourselves be killed. We can't go like beasts to the slaughter. We've got to revolt."

There were a few sturdy young fellows among us. They had knives on them, and they tried to incite the others to throw themselves on the armed guards.

One of the young men cried:

"Let the world learn of the existence of Auschwitz. Let everybody hear about it, while they can still escape. . . ."

But the older ones begged their children not to do anything foolish:

"You must never lose faith, even when the sword hangs over your head. That's the teaching of our sages. . . ."

The wind of revolt died down. We continued our march toward the square. In the middle stood the notorious Dr. Mengele (a typical SS officer: a cruel face, but not devoid of intelligence, and wearing a monocle); a conductor's baton in his hand, he was standing among the other officers. The baton moved unremittingly, sometimes to the right, sometimes to the left.

I was already in front of him:

"How old are you?" he asked, in an attempt at a paternal tone of voice.

"Eighteen." My voice was shaking.

"Are you in good health?"

"Yes."

"What's your occupation?"

Should I say that I was a student?

"Farmer," I heard myself say.

This conversation cannot have lasted more than a few seconds. It had seemed like an eternity to me.

The baton moved to the left. I took half a step forward, I wanted to see first where they were sending my father. If he went to the right, I would go after him.

The baton once again pointed to the left for him, too. A weight was lifted from my heart.

We did not yet know which was the better side, right or left; which road led to prison and which to the crematory. But for the moment I was happy; I was near my father. Our procession continued to move slowly forward.

Another prisoner came up to us:

"Satisfied?"

"Yes," someone replied.

"Poor devils, you're going to the crematory."

He seemed to be telling the truth. Not far from us, flames were leaping up from a ditch, gigantic flames. They were burning something. A lorry drew up at the pit and delivered its load—little children. Babies! Yes, I saw it—saw it with my own eyes . . . those children in the flames. (Is it surprising that I could not sleep after that? Sleep had fled from my eyes.)

So this was where we were going. A little farther on was another and larger ditch for adults.

I pinched my face. Was I still alive? Was I awake? I could not believe it. How could it be possible for them to burn people, children, and for the world to keep silent? No, none of this could be true. It was a nightmare. . . . Soon I should wake with a start, my heart pounding, and find myself back in the bedroom of my childhood, among my books. . . .

My father's voice drew me from my thoughts:

"It's a shame . . . a shame that you couldn't have gone with your mother. . . . I saw several boys of your age going with their mothers. . . ."

His voice was terribly sad. I realized that he did not want to see what they were going to do to me. He did not want to see the burning of his only son.

My forehead was bathed in cold sweat. But I told him that I

did not believe that they could burn people in our age, that humanity would never tolerate it. . . .

"Humanity? Humanity is not concerned with us. Today anything is allowed. Anything is possible, even these crematories. . . ."

His voice was choking.

"Father," I said, "if that is so, I don't want to wait here. I'm going to run to the electric wire. That would be better than slow agony in the flames."

He did not answer. He was weeping. His body was shaken convulsively. Around us, everyone was weeping. Someone began to recite the Kaddish, the prayer for the dead. I do not know if it has ever happened before, in the long history of the Jews, that people have ever recited the prayer for the dead for themselves.

"*Yitgadal veyitkadach shmé; raba.* . . . May His Name be blessed and magnified . . . ," whispered my father.

For the first time, I felt revolt rise up in me. Why should I bless His name? The Eternal, Lord of the Universe, the All-Powerful and Terrible, was silent. What had I to thank Him for?

We continued our march. We were gradually drawing closer to the ditch, from which an infernal heat was rising. Still twenty steps to go. If I wanted to bring about my own death, this was the moment. Our line had now only fifteen paces to cover. I bit my lips so that my father would not hear my teeth chattering. Ten steps still. Eight. Seven. We marched slowly on, as though following a hearse at our own funeral. Four steps more. Three steps. There it was now, right in front of us, the pit and it flames. I gathered all that was left of my strength, so that I could break from the ranks and throw myself upon the barbed wire. In the depths of my heart, I bade farewell to my father, to the whole universe; and, in spite of myself, the words formed themselves and issued in a whisper from my lips: *Yitgadal veyitkadach shmé; raba.* . . . May His name be blessed and magnified. . . . My heart was bursting. The moment had come. I was face to face with the Angel of Death. . . .

No. Two steps from the pit we were ordered to turn to the left and made to go into a barracks.

I pressed my father's hand. He said:

"Do you remember Madame Schächter, in the train?"

Never shall I forget that night, the first night in camp, which has turned my life into one long night, seven times cursed and seven times sealed. Never shall I forget that smoke. Never shall I forget the little faces of the children, whose bodies I saw turned

into wreaths of smoke beneath a silent blue sky.

Never shall I forget those flames which consumed my faith forever.

Never shall I forget that nocturnal silence which deprived me, for all eternity, of the desire to live. Never shall I forget those moments which murdered my God and my soul and turned my dreams to dust. Never shall I forget these things, even if I am condemned to live as long as God Himself. Never.

Eveline

James Joyce

SHE sat at the window watching the evening invade the avenue. Her head was leaned against the window curtains and in her nostrils was the odour of dusty cretonne. She was tired.

Few people passed. The man out of the last house passed on his way home; she heard his footsteps clacking along the concrete pavement and afterwards crunching on the cinder path before the new red houses. One time there used to be a field there in which they used to play every evening with other people's children. Then a man from Belfast bought the field and built houses in it—not like their little brown houses but bright brick houses with shining roofs. The children of the avenue used to play together in that field—the Devines, the Waters, the Dunns, little Keogh the cripple, she and her brothers and sisters. Ernest, however, never played: he was too grown up. Her father used often to hunt them in out of the field with his blackthorn stick; but usually little Keogh used to keep *nix* and call out when he saw her father coming. Still they seemed to have been rather happy then. Her father was not so bad then; and besides, her mother was alive. That was a long time ago; she and her brothers and sisters were all grown up; her mother was dead. Tizzie Dunn was dead, too, and the Waters had gone back to England. Everything changes. Now she was going to go away like the others, to leave her home.

Home! She looked round the room, reviewing all its familiar objects which she had dusted once a week for so many years, wondering where on earth all the dust came from. Perhaps she would never see again those familiar objects from which she had never dreamed of being divided. And yet during all those years she had never found out the name of the priest whose yellowing photograph hung on the wall above the broken harmonium beside the coloured print of the promises made to Blessed Margaret Mary Alacoque. He had been a school friend of her father. Whenever he showed the photograph to a visitor her father used to pass it with a casual word:

—He is in Melbourne now.

She had consented to go away, to leave her home. Was that wise? She tried to weigh each side of the question. In her home

anyway she had shelter and food; she had those whom she had known all her life about her. Of course she had to work hard both in the house and at business. What would they say of her in the Stores when they found out that she had run away with a fellow? Say she was a fool, perhaps; and her place would be filled up by advertisement. Miss Gavan would be glad. She had always had an edge on her, especially whenever there were people listening.

—Miss Hill, don't you see these ladies are waiting?

—Look lively, Miss Hill, please.

She would not cry many tears at leaving the Stores.

But in her new home, in a distant unknown country, it would not be like that. Then she would be married—she, Eveline. People would treat her with respect then. She would not be treated as her mother had been. Even now, though she was over nineteen, she sometimes felt herself in danger of her father's violence. She knew it was that that had given her the palpitations. When they were growing up he had never gone for her, like he used to go for Harry and Ernest, because she was a girl; but latterly he had begun to threaten her and say what he would do to her only for her dead mother's sake. And now she had nobody to protect her. Ernest was dead and Harry, who was in the church decorating business, was nearly always down somewhere in the country. Besides, the invariable squabble for money on Saturday nights had begun to weary her unspeakably. She always gave her entire wages—seven shillings—and Harry always sent up what he could but the trouble was to get any money from her father. He said she used to squander the money, that she had no head, that he wasn't going to give her his hard-earned money to throw about the streets, and much more, for he was usually fairly bad of a Saturday night. In the end he would give her the money and ask her had she any intention of buying Sunday's dinner. Then she had to rush out as quickly as she could and do her marketing, holding her black leather purse tightly in her hand as she elbowed her way through the crowds and returning home late under her load of provisions. She had hard work to keep the house together and to see that the two young children who had been left to her charge went to school regularly and got their meals regularly. It was hard work—a hard life—but now that she was about to leave it she did not find it a wholly undesirable life.

She was about to explore another life with Frank. Frank was very kind, manly, open-hearted. She was to go away with him by the night-boat to be his wife and to live with him in Buenos Ayres where he had a home waiting for her. How well she re-

membered the first time she had seen him; he was lodging in a house on the main road where she used to visit. It seemed a few weeks ago. He was standing at the gate, his peaked cap pushed back on his head and his hair tumbled forward over a face of bronze. Then they had come to know each other. He used to meet her outside the Stores every evening and see her home. He took her to see *The Bohemian Girl* and she felt elated as she sat in an unaccustomed part of the theatre with him. He was awfully fond of music and sang a little. People knew that they were courting and, when he sang about the lass that loves a sailor, she always felt pleasantly confused. He used to call her Poppens out of fun. First of all it had been an excitement for her to have a fellow and then she had begun to like him. He had tales of distant countries. He had started as a deck boy at a pound a month on a ship of the Allan Line going out to Canada. He told her the names of the ships he had been on and the names of the different services. He had sailed through the Straits of Magellan and he told her stories of the terrible Patagonians. He had fallen on his feet in Buenos Ayres, he said, and had come over to the old country just for a holiday. Of course, her father had found out the affair and had forbidden her to have anything to say to him.

—I know these sailor chaps, he said.

One day he had quarrelled with Frank and after that she had to meet her lover secretly.

The evening deepened in the avenue. The white of two letters in her lap grew indistinct. One was to Harry; the other was to her father. Ernest had been her favourite but she liked Harry too. Her father was becoming old lately, she noticed; he would miss her. Sometimes he could be very nice. Not long before, when she had been laid up for a day, he had read her out a ghost story and made toast for her at the fire. Another day, when their mother was alive, they had all gone for a picnic to the Hill of Howth. She remembered her father putting on her mother's bonnet to make the children laugh.

Her time was running out but she continued to sit by the window, leaning her head against the window curtain, inhaling the odour of dusty cretonne. Down far in the avenue she could hear a street organ playing. She knew the air. Strange that it should come that very night to remind her of the promise to her mother, her promise to keep the home together as long as she could. She remembered the last night of her mother's illness; she was again in the close dark room at the other side of the hall and outside she heard a melancholy air of Italy. The organ-

player had been ordered to go away and given sixpence. She remembered her father strutting back into the sickroom saying:

—Damned Italians! coming over here!

As she mused the pitiful vision of her mother's life laid its spell on the very quick of her being—that life of commonplace sacrifices closing in final craziness. She trembled as she heard again her mother's voice saying constantly with foolish insistence:

—Derevaun Seraun! Derevaun Seraun!

She stood up in a sudden impulse of terror. Escape! She must escape! Frank would save her. He would give her life, perhaps love, too. But she wanted to live. Why should she be unhappy? She had a right to happiness. Frank would take her in his arms, fold her in his arms. He would save her.

She stood among the swaying crowd in the station at the North Wall. He held her hand and she knew that he was speaking to her, saying something about the passage over and over again. The station was full of soldiers with brown baggages. Through the wide doors of the sheds she caught a glimpse of the black mass of the boat, lying in beside the quay wall, with illumined portholes. She answered nothing. She felt her cheek pale and cold and, out of a maze of distress, she prayed to God to direct her, to show her what was her duty. The boat blew a long mournful whistle into the mist. If she went, to-morrow she would be on the sea with Frank, steaming towards Buenos Ayres. Their passage had been booked. Could she still draw back after all he had done for her? Her distress awoke a nausea in her body and she kept moving her lips in silent fervent prayer.

A bell clanged upon her heart. She felt him seize her hand:

—Come!

All the seas of the world tumbled about her heart. He was drawing her into them: he would drown her. She gripped with both hands at the iron railing.

—Come!

No! No! No! It was impossible. Her hands clutched the iron in frenzy. Amid the seas she sent a cry of anguish!

—Eveline! Evvy!

He rushed beyond the barrier and called to her to follow. He was shouted at to go on but he still called to her. She set her white face to him, passive, like a helpless animal. Her eyes gave him no sign of love or farewell or recognition.

The Swan

Rainer Maria Rilke

Translated by Robert Bly

This clumsy living that moves lumbering
as if in ropes through what is not done
reminds us of the awkward way the swan walks.

And to die, which is a letting go
of the ground we stand on and cling to every day,
is like the swan when he nervously lets himself down

into the water, which receives him gaily
and which flows joyfully under
and after him, wave after wave,
while the swan, unmoving and marvelously calm,
is pleased to be carried, each minute more fully grown,
more like a king, composed, farther and farther on.

Tale of the Computer
That Fought a Dragon

Stanislaw Łem

KING Poleander Partobon, ruler of Cyberia, was a great warrior, and being an advocate of the methods of modern strategy, above all else he prized cybernetics as a military art. His kingdom swarmed with thinking machines, for Poleander put them everywhere he could; not merely in the astronomical observatories or the schools, but he ordered electric brains mounted in the rocks upon the roads, which with loud voices cautioned pedestrians against tripping; also in posts, in walls, in trees, so that one could ask directions anywhere when lost; he stuck them onto clouds, so they could announce the rain in advance, he added them to the hills and valleys—in short, it was impossible to walk on Cyberia without bumping into an intelligent machine. The planet was beautiful, since the King not only gave decrees for the cybernetic perfecting of that which had long been in existence, but he introduced by law entirely new orders of things. Thus for example in his kingdom were manufactured cyberbeetles and buzzing cyberbees, and even cyberflies—these would be seized by mechanical spiders when they grew too numerous. On the planet cyberbosks of cybergorse rustled in the wind, cybercalliopes and cyberviols sang—but besides these civilian devices there were twice as many military, for the King was most bellicose. In his palace vaults he had a strategic computer, a machine of uncommon mettle; he had smaller ones also, and divisions of cybersaries, enormous cybermatics and a whole arsenal of every other kind of weapon, including powder. There was only this one problem, and it troubled him greatly, namely, that he had not a single adversary or enemy and no one in any way wished to invade his land and thereby provide him with the opportunity to demonstrate his kingly and terrifying courage, his tactical genius, not to mention the simply extraordinary effectiveness of his cybernetic weaponry. In the absence of genuine enemies and aggressors, the King had his engineers build artificial ones, and against these he did battle and always won. However, inasmuch as the battles and campaigns were genuinely dreadful, the populace suffered no little injury from them. The

subjects murmured when all too many cyberfoes had destroyed their settlements and towns, when the synthetic enemy poured liquid fire upon them; they even dared voice their discontent when the King himself, issuing forth as their deliverer and vanquishing the artificial foe, in the course of the victorious attacks laid waste to everything that stood in his path. They grumbled even then, the ingrates, though the thing was done on their behalf.

Until the King wearied of the war games on the planet and decided to raise his sights. Now it was cosmic wars and sallies that he dreamed of. His planet had a large Moon, entirely desolate and wild; the King laid heavy taxes upon his subjects to obtain the funds needed to build whole armies on that Moon and have there a new theater of war. And the subjects were more than happy to pay, figuring that King Poleander would now no longer deliver them with his cybermatics nor test the strength of his arms upon their homes and heads. And so the royal engineers built on the Moon a splendid computer, which in turn was to create all manner of troops and self-firing gunnery. The King lost no time in testing the machine's prowess this way and that; at one point he ordered it—by telegraph—to execute a volt-vault electrosault: for he wanted to see if it was true, what his engineers had told him, that that machine could do anything. If it can do anything, he thought, then let it do a flip. However, the text of the telegram underwent a slight distortion and the machine received the order that it was to execute not an electrosault, but an electrosaur— and this it carried out as best it could.

Meanwhile the King conducted one more campaign, liberating some provinces of his realm seized by cyberknechts; he completely forgot about the order given the computer on the Moon— then suddenly giant boulders came hurtling down from there; the King was astounded, for one even fell on the wing of the palace and destroyed his prize collection of cyberads, which are dryads with feedback. Fuming, he telegraphed the Moon computer at once, demanding an explanation. It didn't reply, however, for it no longer was: the electrosaur had swallowed it and made it into its own tail.

Immediately the King dispatched an entire armed expedition to the Moon, placing at its head another computer, also very valiant, to slay the dragon, but there was only some flashing, some rumbling, and then no more computer nor expedition; for the electrodragon wasn't pretend and wasn't pretending, but battled with the utmost verisimilitude, and had moreover the worst of inten-

tions regarding the kingdom and the King. The King sent to the Moon his cybernants, cyberneers, cyberines and lieutenant cybernets; at the very end he even sent one cyberalissimo, but it too accomplished nothing; the hurly-burly lasted a little longer, that was all. The King watched through a telescope set up on the palace balcony.

The dragon grew; the Moon became smaller and smaller, since the monster was devouring it piecemeal and incorporating it into its own body. The King saw then, and his subjects did also, that things were serious, for when the ground beneath the feet of the electrosaur was gone, it would for certain hurl itself upon the planet and upon them. The King thought and thought, but he saw no remedy and knew not what to do. To send machines was no good, for they would be lost, and to go himself was no better, for he was afraid. Suddenly the King heard, in the stillness of the night, the telegraph chattering from his royal bedchamber. It was the King's personal receiver, solid gold with a diamond needle, linked to the Moon; the King jumped up and ran to it; the apparatus meanwhile went *tap-tap, tap-tap,* and tapped out this telegram: THE DRAGON SAYS POLEANDER PARTOBON BETTER CLEAR OUT BECAUSE HE THE DRAGON INTENDS TO OCCUPY THE THRONE!

The King took fright, quaked from head to toe, and ran, just as he was, in his ermine nightshirt and slippers, down to the palace vaults, where stood the strategy machine, old and very wise. He had not as yet consulted it, since prior to the rise and uprise of the electrodragon they had argued on the subject of a certain military operation; but now was not the time to think of that— his throne, his life was at stake!

He plugged it in, and as soon as it warmed up he cried:

"My old computer! My good computer! It's this way and that, the dragon wishes to deprive me of my throne, to cast me out, help, speak, how can I defeat it?!"

"Uh-uh," said the computer. "First you must admit I was right in that previous business, and secondly, I would have you address me only as Digital Grand Vizier, though you may also say to me: `Your Ferromagneticity!'"

"Good, good, I'll name you Grand Vizier, I'll agree to anything you like, only save me!"

The machine whirred, chirred, hummed, hemmed, then said:

"It is a simple matter. We build an electrosaur more powerful than the one located on the Moon. It will defeat the lunar one,

settle its circuitry once and for all and thereby attain the goal!"

"Perfect!" replied the King. "And can you make a blueprint of this dragon?"

"It will be an ultradragon," said the computer. "And I can make you not only a blueprint, but the thing itself, which I shall now do; it won't take a minute, King!" And true to its word, it hissed, it chugged, it whistled and buzzed, assembling something down within itself, and already an object like a giant claw, sparking, arcing, was emerging from its side, when the King shouted:

"Old computer! Stop!"

"Is this how you address me? I am the Digital Grand Vizier!"

"Ah, of course," said the King. "Your Ferromagneticity, the electrodragon you are making will defeat the other dragon, granted, but it will surely remain in the other's place. How then are we to get rid of it in turn?!"

"By making yet another, still more powerful," explained the computer.

"No, no! In that case don't do anything, I beg you. What good will it be to have more and more terrible dragons on the Moon when I don't want any there at all?"

"Ah, now that's a different matter," the computer replied. "Why didn't you say so in the first place? You see how illogically you express yourself? One moment . . . I must think."

And it churred and hummed, and chuffed and chuckled, and finally said:

"We make an antimoon with an antidragon, place it in the Moon's orbit (here something went snap inside), sit around the fire and sing: *Oh, I'm a robot full of fun, water doesn't scare me none, I dives right in, I gives a grin, tra la the livelong day!!*"

"You speak strangely," said the King. "What does the antimoon have to do with that song about the funny robot?"

"What funny robot?" asked the computer. "Ah, no, no, I made a mistake, something feels wrong inside, I must have blown a tube." The King began to look for the trouble, finally found the burnt out tube, put in a new one, then asked the computer about the antimoon.

"What antimoon?" asked the computer, which meanwhile had forgotten what it said before. "I don't know anything about an antimoon . . . one moment, I have to give this thought."

It hummed, it huffed, and it said:

"We create a general theory of the slaying of electrodragons, of which the lunar dragon will be a special case, its solution trivial."

"Well, create such a theory!" said the King.

"To do this I must first create various experimental dragons."

"Certainly not! No thank you!" exclaimed the King. "A dragon wants to deprive me of my throne. Just think what might happen if you produced a swarm of them!"

"Oh? Well then, in that case we must resort to other means. We will use a strategic variant of the method of successive approximations. Go and telegraph the dragon that you will give it the throne on the condition that it perform three mathematical operations, really quite simple . . ."

The King went and telegraphed, and the dragon agreed. The King returned to the computer.

"Now," it said, "here is the first operation: tell it to divide itself by itself!"

The King did this. The electrosaur divided itself by itself, but since one electrosaur over one electrosaur is one, it remained on the Moon and nothing changed.

"Is this the best you can do?!" cried the King, running into the vault with such haste that his slippers fell off. "The dragon divided itself by itself, but since one goes into one once, nothing changed!"

"That's all right. I did that on purpose—the operation was to divert attention," said the computer. "And now tell it to extract its root!" The King telegraphed to the Moon, and the dragon began to pull, push, pull, push, until it crackled from the strain, panted, trembled all over, but suddenly something gave—and it extracted its own root!

The King went back to the computer.

"The dragon crackled, trembled, even ground its teeth, but extracted the root and threatens me still!" he shouted from the doorway. "What now, my old . . . I mean, Your Ferromagneticity?!"

"Be of stout heart," it said. "Now go tell it to subtract itself from itself!"

The King hurried to his royal bedchamber, sent the telegram, and the dragon began to subtract itself from itself, taking away its tail first, then legs, then trunk, and finally, when it saw that something wasn't right, it hesitated, but from its own momentum the subtracting continued, it took away its head and became zero, in other words, nothing: the electrosaur was no more!

"The electrosaur is no more," cried the joyful King, bursting into the vault. "Thank you, old computer . . . many thanks . . . you have worked hard . . . you have earned a rest, so now I will disconnect you."

"Not so fast, my dear," the computer replied. "I do the job and you want to disconnect me, and you no longer call me Your Ferromagneticity?! That's not nice, not nice at all! Now I myself will change into an electrosaur, yes, and drive you from the kingdom, and most certainly rule better than you, for you always consulted me in all the more important matters; therefore, it was really I who ruled all along, and not you . . ."

And huffing, puffing, it began to change into an electrosaur; flaming electroclaws were already protruding from its sides when the King, breathless with fright, tore the slippers off his feet, rushed up to it and with the slippers began beating blindly at its tubes! The computer chugged, choked, and got muddled in its program—instead of the word "electrosaur" it read "electrosauce," and before the King's very eyes the computer, wheezing more and more softly, turned into an enormous, gleaming-golden heap of electrosauce, which, still sizzling, emitted all its charge in deep blue sparks, leaving Poleander to stare dumbstruck at only a great, steaming pool of gravy . . .

With a sigh the King put on his slippers and returned to the royal bedchamber. However, from that time on he was an altogether different king: the events he had undergone made his nature less bellicose, and to the end of his days he engaged exclusively in civilian cybernetics and left the military kind strictly alone.

Weightless

Primo Levi

Translated by Piers Spence

WHAT I would like to experience most of all would be to find myself freed, even if only for a moment, from the weight of my body. I wouldn't want to overdo it—just to hang suspended for a reasonable period—and yet I feel intensely envious of those weightless astronauts whom we are permitted to see all too rarely on our TV screens. They seem as much at ease as fish in water: they move elegantly around their cockpit—these days quite spacious—propelling themselves forward by pushing gently off invisible walls, and sailing smoothly through the air to berth securely at their work place. At other times we have seen them conversing, as if it were the most natural thing—one of them "the right way up," the other "upside down" (but of course in orbit there is neither up nor down). Or we have seen them take turns to play childish games: one flicks a toffee with his thumbnail, and it flies slowly and in a perfectly straight line into the open mouth of his colleague. We have seen an astronaut squirt water from a plastic container into the air: the water does not fall or disperse but settles in a roundish mass which then, subject only to the weak forces of surface tension, lazily assumes the form of a sphere. What do they do with it then? It can't be easy to dispose of without damaging the delicate structures upholding its surface.

I wonder what it would take to make a documentary that would link together these visions, transmitted by some miracle from the satellites that flash past above our heads and above our atmosphere. A film like that, drawn from American and Soviet sources, and with an intelligent commentary, would teach everybody so much. It would certainly be more successful than the nonsense that is put out today.

I have also often wondered about the experiments, or more particularly the simulation courses which aspiring astronauts have to undergo and which journalists write about as if they were nothing out of the ordinary. What sense is there in them? And how is weightlessness simulated? The only technique imaginable would be to close the candidates in a vehicle in free-fall: a

plane or an elevator such as Einstein postulated for the experiment designed to illustrate the concept of special relativity. But a plane, even in a vertical fall, is braked by the resistance of the air, and a lift (or rather, a fall) has additional frictional forces acting on the cable. In both cases, weightlessness (or *abaria* to the die-hard classicists) would not be complete. And even in the best case—the quite terrifying scenario of a plane dropping like a stone from a height of five or ten or twenty miles, perhaps with an additional thrust from the engines in the final stages—the whole thing would last no more than a few tens of seconds: not enough time for any training or for measuring physiological data. And then there would be the question of stopping . . .

And yet almost all of us have experienced a "simulation" of this decidedly non-terrestrial sensation. We have felt it in a childhood dream. In the most typical version, the dreamer becomes aware with joyous amazement that flying is as easy as walking or swimming. How could you have been so stupid as not to have thought of it before? You just scull with the palms of your hands and—hey presto—you take off from the floor, moving effortlessly; you turn around, avoiding the obstacles; you pass skillfully through doors and windows, and escape into the open air: not with the frenetic whirring of a sparrow's wings, not with the voracious, stridulant haste of a swallow, but with the silent majesty of the eagles and the clouds. Where does this presentiment of what is now a concrete reality come from? Perhaps it is a memory common to the species, inherited from our proto-bird-like aquatic reptiles. Or maybe this dream is a prelude to the future, as yet unclear, in which the umbilical cord which calls us back to mother earth will be superfluous and transparent: the advent of a new mode of locomotion, more noble even than our own complicated, unsteady, two-legged style with its internal inefficiencies and its need of external friction between the feet and the ground.

From this persistent dream of weightlessness, my mind returns to a well-known rendition of the Geryon episode in the seventeenth canto of the *Inferno*. The "wild beast," reconstructed by Dante from classical sources and also from word-of-mouth accounts of the medieval bestiaries, is imaginary and at the same time splendidly real. It eludes the burden of weight. Waiting for its two strange passengers, only one of whom is subject to the laws of gravity, the wild beast rests on the bank with its forelegs, but its deadly tail floats "in the void" like the stern-

end of a Zeppelin moored to its pylon. At first, Dante was frightened by the creature, but then that magical descent to Malebolge captured the attention of the poet-scientist, paradoxically absorbed in the naturalistic study of his fictional beast whose monstrous and symbolic form he describes with precision. The brief description of the journey on the back of the beast is singularly accurate, down to the details as confirmed by the pilots of modern hang-gliders: the silent, gliding flight, where the passenger's perception of speed is not informed by the rhythm or the noise of the wings but only by the sensation of the air which is "on their face and from below." Perhaps Dante, too, was reproducing here unconsciously the universal dream of weightless flight, to which psychoanalysts attribute problematical and immodest significance.

The ease with which man adapts to weightlessness is a fascinating mystery. Considering that for many people travel by sea or even by car can cause bouts of nausea, one can't help feeling perplexed. During month-long spells in space the astronauts complained only of passing discomforts, and doctors who examined them afterwards discovered a light decalcification of the bones and a transitory atrophy of the heart muscles: the same effects, in other words, produced by a period of confinement to bed. Yet nothing in our long history of evolution could have prepared us for a condition as unnatural as non-gravity.

Thus we have vast and unforeseen margins of safety: the visionary idea of humanity migrating from star to star on vessels with huge sails driven by stellar light might have limits, but not that of weightlessness: our poor body, so vulnerable to swords, to guns and to viruses, is space-proof.

Lot's Wife

Anna Akhmatova

Translated by Judith Hemschemeyer

And the righteous man followed the envoy of God,
Huge and bright, over the black mountain.
But anguish spoke loudly to his wife:
It is not too late, you can still gaze

At the red towers of your native Sodom,
At the square where you sang, at the courtyard where you
   spun,
At the empty windows of the tall house
Where you bore children to your beloved husband.

She glanced, and, paralyzed by deadly pain,
Her eyes no longer saw anything;
And her body became transparent salt
And her quick feet were rooted to the spot.

Who will weep for this woman?
Isn't her death the least significant?
But my heart will never forget the one
Who gave her life for a single glance.

The Guest

Albert Camus

Translated by Justin O'Brien

THE schoolmaster was watching the two men climb toward him. One was on horseback, the other on foot. They had not yet tackled the abrupt rise leading to the schoolhouse built on the hillside. They were toiling onward, making slow progress in the snow, among the stones, on the vast expanse of the high, deserted plateau. From time to time the horse stumbled. Without hearing anything yet, he could see the breath issuing from the horse's nostrils. One of the men, at least, knew the region. They were following the trail although it had disappeared days ago under a layer of dirty white snow. The schoolmaster calculated that it would take them half an hour to get onto the hill. It was cold; he went back into the school to get a sweater.

He crossed the empty, frigid classroom. On the blackboard the four rivers of France, drawn with four different colored chalks, had been flowing toward their estuaries for the past three days. Snow had suddenly fallen in mid-October after eight months of drought without the transition of rain, and the twenty pupils, more or less, who lived in the villages scattered over the plateau had stopped coming. With fair weather they would return. Daru now heated only the single room that was his lodging, adjoining the classroom and giving also onto the plateau to the east. Like the class windows, his window looked to the south, too. On that side the school was a few kilometers from the point where the plateau began to slope toward the south. In clear weather could be seen the purple mass of the mountain range where the gap opened onto the desert.

Somewhat warmed, Daru returned to the window from which he had first seen the two men. They were no longer visible. Hence they must have tackled the rise. The sky was not so dark, for the snow had stopped falling during the night. The morning had opened with a dirty light which had scarcely become brighter as the ceiling of clouds lifted. At two in the afternoon it seemed as if the day were merely beginning. But still this was better than those three days when the thick snow was falling amidst unbroken darkness with little gusts of wind that rattled the double door

of the classroom. Then Daru had spent long hours in his room, leaving it only to go to the shed and feed the chickens or get some coal. Fortunately the delivery truck from Tadjid, the nearest village to the north, had brought his supplies two days before the blizzard. It would return in forty-eight hours.

Besides, he had enough to resist a siege, for the little room was cluttered with bags of wheat that the administration left as a stock to distribute to those of his pupils whose families had suffered from the drought. Actually they had all been victims because they were all poor. Everyday Daru would distribute a ration to the children. They had missed it, he knew, during these bad days. Possibly one of the fathers or big brothers would come this afternoon and he could supply them with grain. It was just a matter of carrying them over to the next harvest. Now shiploads of wheat were arriving from France and the worst was over. But it would be hard to forget that poverty, that army of ragged ghosts wandering in the sunlight, the plateaus burned to a cinder month after month, the earth shriveled up little by little, literally scorched, every stone bursting into dust under one's foot. The sheep had died then by thousands and even a few men, here and there, sometimes without anyone's knowing.

In contrast with such poverty, he who lived almost like a monk in his remote schoolhouse, nonetheless satisfied with the little he had and with the rough life, had felt like a lord with his white-washed walls, his narrow couch, his unpainted shelves, his well, and his weekly provision of water and food. And suddenly this snow, without warning, without the foretaste of rain. This is the way the region was, cruel to live in, even without men—who didn't help matters either. But Daru had been born here. Everywhere else, he felt exiled.

He stepped out onto the terrace in front of the schoolhouse. The two men were now halfway up the slope. He recognized the horseman as Balducci, the old gendarme he had known for a long time. Balducci was holding on the end of a rope an Arab who was walking behind him with hands bound and head lowered. The gendarme waved a greeting to which Daru did not reply, lost as he was in contemplation of the Arab dressed in a faded blue djellaba, his feet in sandals but covered with socks of heavy raw wool, his head surmounted by a narrow, short *chèche*. They were approaching. Balducci was holding back his horse in order not to hurt the Arab, and the group was advancing slowly.

31

Within earshot, Balducci shouted: "One hour to do the three kilometers from El Ameur!" Daru did not answer. Short and square in his thick sweater, he watched them climb. Not once had the Arab raised his head. "Hello," said Daru when they got up onto the terrace. "Come in and warm up." Balducci painfully got down from his horse without letting go the rope. From under his bristling mustache he smiled at the schoolmaster. His little dark eyes, deep set under a tanned forehead, and his mouth surrounded with wrinkles made him look attentive and studious. Daru took the bridle, led the horse to the shed, and came back to the two men, who were now waiting for him in the school. He led them into his room. "I am going to heat up the classroom," he said. "We'll be more comfortable there." When he entered the room again, Balducci was on the couch. He had undone the rope tying him to the Arab, who had squatted near the stove. His hands still bound, the *chèche* pushed back on his head, he was looking toward the window. At first Daru noticed only his huge lips, fat, smooth, almost Negroid; yet his nose was straight, his eyes were dark and full of fever. The *chèche* revealed an obstinate forehead and, under the weathered skin now rather discolored by the cold, the whole face had a restless and rebellious look that struck Daru when the Arab, turning his face toward him, looked him straight in the eyes. "Go into the other room," said the schoolmaster, "and I'll make you some mint tea." "Thanks," Balducci said. "What a chore! How I long for retirement." And addressing his prisoner in Arabic: "Come on, you." The Arab got up and, slowly, holding his bound wrists in front of him, went into the classroom.

With the tea, Daru brought a chair. But Balducci was already enthroned on the nearest pupil's desk and the Arab had squatted against the teacher's platform facing the stove, which stood between the desk and the window. When he held out the glass of tea to the prisoner, Daru hesitated at the sight of his bound hands. "He might perhaps be untied." "Sure," said Balducci. "That was for the trip." He started to get to his feet. But Daru, setting the glass on the floor, had knelt beside the Arab. Without saying anything, the Arab watched him with his feverish eyes. Once his hands were free, he rubbed his swollen wrists against each other, took the glass of tea, and sucked up the burning liquid in swift little sips.

"Good," said Daru. "And where are you headed?"

Balducci withdrew his mustache from the tea. "Here, son."

"Odd pupils! And you're spending the night?"

"No. I'm going back to El Ameur. And you will deliver this fellow to Tinguit. He is expected at police headquarters."

Balducci was looking at Daru with a friendly little smile.

"What's this story?" asked the schoolmaster. "Are you pulling my leg?"

"No, son. Those are the orders."

"The orders? I'm not . . ." Daru hesitated, not wanting to hurt the old Corsican. "I mean, that's not my job."

"What! What's the meaning of that? In wartime people do all kinds of jobs."

"Then I'll wait for the declaration of war."

Balducci nodded.

"O.K. But the orders exist and they concern you, too. Things are brewing, it appears. There is talk of a forthcoming revolt. We are mobilized, in a way."

Daru still had his obstinate look.

"Listen, son," Balducci said. "I like you and you must understand. There's only a dozen of us at El Ameur to patrol throughout the whole territory of a small department and I must get back in a hurry. I was told to hand this guy over to you and return without delay. He couldn't be kept there. His village was beginning to stir; they wanted to take him back. You must take him to Tinguit tomorrow before the day is over. Twenty kilometers shouldn't faze a husky fellow like you. After that, all will be over. You'll come back to your pupils and your comfortable life."

Behind the wall the horse could be heard snorting and pawing the earth. Daru was looking out the window. Decidedly, the weather was clearing and the light was increasing over the snowy plateau. When all the snow was melted, the sun would take over again and once more would burn the fields of stone. For days, still, the unchanging sky would shed its dry light on the solitary expanse where nothing had any connection with man.

"After all," he said, turning around toward Balducci, "what did he do?" And, before the gendarme had opened his mouth, he asked: "Does he speak French?"

"No, not a word. We had been looking for him for a month, but they were hiding him. He killed his cousin."

"Is he against us?"

"I don't think so. But you can never be sure."

"Why did he kill?"

"A family squabble, I think. One owed the other grain, it seems. It's not at all clear. In short, he killed his cousin with a billhook. You know, like a sheep, *kreezk!*"

Balducci made the gesture of drawing a blade across his throat and the Arab, his attention attracted, watched him with a sort of anxiety. Daru felt a sudden wrath against the man, against all men with their rotten spite, their tireless hates, their blood lust.

But the kettle was singing on the stove. He served Balducci more tea, hesitated, then served the Arab again, who, a second time, drank avidly. His raised arms made the djellaba fall open and the schoolmaster saw his thin, muscular chest.

"Thanks, kid," Balducci said. "And now, I'm off."

He got up and went toward the Arab, taking a small rope from his pocket.

"What are you doing?" Daru asked dryly.

Balducci, disconcerted, showed him the rope.

"Don't bother."

The old gendarme hesitated. "It's up to you. Of course, you are armed?"

"I have my shotgun."

"Where?"

"In the trunk."

"You ought to have it near your bed."

"Why? I have nothing to fear."

"You're crazy, son. If there's an uprising, no one is safe, we're all in the same boat."

"I'll defend myself. I'll have time to see them coming."

Balducci began to laugh, then suddenly the mustache covered the white teeth.

"You'll have time? O.K. That's just what I was saying. You have always been a little cracked. That's why I like you, my son was like that."

At the same time he took out his revolver and put it on the desk.

"Keep it; I don't need two weapons from here to El Ameur."

The revolver shone against the black paint of the table. When the gendarme turned toward him, the schoolmaster caught the smell of leather and horseflesh.

"Listen, Balducci," Daru said suddenly, "every bit of this disgusts me, and first of all your fellow here. But I won't hand him over. Fight, yes, if I have to. But not that."

The old gendarme stood in front of him and looked at him severely.

"You're being a fool," he said slowly. "I don't like it either. You don't get used to putting a rope on a man even after years of it, and you're even ashamed—yes, ashamed. But you can't let them have their way."

"I won't hand him over," Daru said again.

"It's an order, son, and I repeat it."

"That's right. Repeat to them what I've said to you: I won't hand him over."

Balducci made a visible effort to reflect. He looked at the Arab and at Daru. At last he decided.

"No, I won't tell them anything. If you want to drop us, go ahead; I'll not denounce you. I have an order to deliver the prisoner and I'm doing so. And now you'll just sign this paper for me."

"There's no need. I'll not deny that you left him with me."

"Don't be mean with me. I know you'll tell the truth. You're from hereabouts and you are a man. But you must sign, that's the rule."

Daru opened his drawer, took out a little square bottle of purple ink, the red wooden penholder with the "sergeant-major" pen he used for making models of penmanship, and signed. The gendarme carefully folded the paper and put it into his wallet. Then he moved toward the door.

"I'll see you off," Daru said.

"No," said Balducci. "There's no use being polite. You insulted me."

He looked at the Arab, motionless in the same spot, sniffed peevishly, and turned away toward the door. "Goodbye, son," he said. The door shut behind him. Balducci appeared suddenly outside the window and then disappeared. His footsteps were muffled by the snow. The horse stirred on the other side of the wall and several chickens fluttered in fright. A moment later Balducci reappeared outside the window leading the horse by the bridle. He walked toward the little rise without turning around and disappeared from sight with the horse following him. A big stone could be heard bouncing down. Daru walked back toward the prisoner, who, without stirring, never took his eyes off him. "Wait," the schoolmaster said in Arabic and went toward the bedroom. As he was going through the door, he had a second thought, went to the desk, took the revolver, and stuck it in his pocket. Then, without looking back, he went into his room.

For some time he lay on his couch watching the sky gradually close over, listening to the silence. It was this silence that had

seemed painful to him during the first days here, after the war. He had requested a post in the little town at the base of the foothills separating the upper plateaus from the desert. There, rocky walls, green and black to the north, pink and lavender to the south, marked the frontier of eternal summer. He had been named to a post farther north, on the plateau itself. In the beginning, the solitude and the silence had been hard for him on these wastelands peopled only by stones. Occasionally, furrows suggested cultivation, but they had been dug to uncover a certain kind of stone good for building. The only plowing here was to harvest rocks. Elsewhere a thin layer of soil accumulated in the hollows would be scraped out to enrich paltry village gardens. This is the way it was: bare rock covered three quarters of the region. Towns sprang up, flourished, then disappeared; men came by, loved one another or fought bitterly, then died. No one in this desert, neither he nor his guest, mattered. And yet, outside this desert neither of them, Daru knew, could have really lived.

When he got up, no noise came from the classroom. He was amazed at the unmixed joy he derived from the mere thought that the Arab might have fled and that he would be alone with no decision to make. But the prisoner was there. He had merely stretched out between the stove and the desk. With eyes open, he was staring at the ceiling. In that position, his thick lips were particularly noticeable, giving him a pouting look. "Come," said Daru. The Arab got up and followed him. In the bedroom, the schoolmaster pointed to a chair near the table under the window. The Arab sat down without taking his eyes off Daru.

"Are you hungry?"

"Yes," the prisoner said.

Daru set the table for two. He took flour and oil, shaped a cake in a frying pan, and lighted the little stove that functioned on bottled gas. While the cake was cooking, he went out to the shed to get cheese, eggs, dates, and condensed milk. When the cake was done he set it on the window sill to cool, heated some condensed milk diluted with water, and beat up the eggs into an omelette. In one of his motions he knocked against the revolver stuck in his right pocket. He set the bowl down, went into the classroom, and put the revolver in his desk drawer. When he came back to the room, night was falling. He put on the light and served the Arab. "Eat," he said. The Arab took a piece of the cake, lifted it eagerly to his mouth, and stopped short.

"And you?" he asked.

"After you. I'll eat, too."

The thick lips opened slightly. The Arab hesitated, then bit into the cake determinedly.

The meal over, the Arab looked at the schoolmaster. "Are you the judge?"

"No, I'm simply keeping you until tomorrow."

"Why do you eat with me?"

"I'm hungry."

The Arab fell silent. Daru got up and went out. He brought back a folding bed from the shed, set it up between the table and the stove, perpendicular to his own bed. From a large suitcase which, upright in a corner, served as a shelf for papers, he took two blankets and arranged them on the camp bed. Then he stopped, felt useless, and sat down on his bed. There was nothing more to do or to get ready. He had to look at this man. He looked at him, therefore, trying to imagine his face bursting with rage. He couldn't do so. He could see nothing but the dark yet shining eyes and the animal mouth.

"Why did you kill him?" he asked in a voice whose hostile tone surprised him.

The Arab looked away.

"He ran away. I ran after him."

He raised his eyes to Daru again and they were full of a sort of woeful interrogation. "Now what will they do to me?"

"Are you afraid?"

He stiffened, turning his eyes away.

"Are you sorry?"

The Arab stared at him openmouthed. Obviously he did not understand. Daru's annoyance was growing. At the same time he felt awkward and self-conscious with his big body wedged between the two beds.

"Lie down there," he said impatiently. "That's your bed."

The Arab didn't move. He called to Daru: "Tell me!"

The schoolmaster looked at him.

"Is the gendarme coming back tomorrow?"

"I don't know."

"Are you coming with us?"

"I don't know. Why?"

The prisoner got up and stretched out on top of the blankets, his feet toward the window. The light from the electric bulb shone straight into his eyes and he closed them at once.

"Why?" Daru repeated, standing beside the bed.

The Arab opened his eyes under the blinding light and looked at him, trying not to blink.

"Come with us," he said.

In the middle of the night, Daru was still not asleep. He had gone to bed after undressing completely; he generally slept naked. But when he suddenly realized that he had nothing on, he hesitated. He felt vulnerable and the temptation came to him to put his clothes back on. Then he shrugged his shoulders; after all, he wasn't a child and, if need be, he could break his adversary in two. From his bed he could observe him, lying on his back, still motionless with his eyes closed under the harsh light. When Daru turned out the light, the darkness seemed to coagulate all of a sudden. Little by little, the night came back to life in the window where the starless sky was stirring gently. The schoolmaster soon made out the body lying at his feet. The Arab still did not move, but his eyes seemed open. A faint wind was prowling around the schoolhouse. Perhaps it would drive away the clouds and the sun would reappear.

During the night the wind increased. The hens fluttered a little and then were silent. The Arab turned over on his side with his back to Daru, who thought he heard him moan. Then he listened for his guest's breathing become heavier and more regular. He listened to that breath so close to him and mused without being able to go to sleep. In this room where he had been sleeping alone for a year, this presence bothered him. But it bothered him also by imposing on him a sort of brotherhood he knew well but refused to accept in the present circumstances. Men who share the same rooms, soldiers or prisoners, develop a strange alliance as if, having cast off their armor with their clothing, they fraternized every evening, over and above their differences, in the ancient community of dream and fatigue. But Daru shook himself; he didn't like such musings, and it was essential to sleep.

A little later, however, when the Arab stirred slightly, the schoolmaster was still not asleep. When the prisoner made a second move, he stiffened, on the alert. The Arab was lifting himself slowly on his arms with almost the motion of a sleepwalker. Seated upright in bed, he waited motionless without turning his head toward Daru, as if he were listening attentively. Daru did not stir; it had just occurred to him that the revolver was still in the drawer of his desk. It was better to act at once. Yet he continued to observe the prisoner, who, with the

same slithery motion, put his feet on the ground, waited again, then began to stand up slowly. Daru was about to call out to him when the Arab began to walk, in a quite natural but extraordinarily silent way. He was heading toward the door at the end of the room that opened into the shed. He lifted the latch with precaution and went out, pushing the door behind him but without shutting it. Daru had not stirred. "He is running away," he merely thought. "Good riddance!" Yet he listened attentively. The hens were not fluttering; the guest must be on the plateau. A faint sound of water reached him, and he didn't know what it was until the Arab again stood framed in the doorway, closed the door carefully, and came back to bed without a sound. Then Daru turned his back on him and fell asleep. Still later he seemed, from the depths of his sleep, to hear furtive steps around the schoolhouse. "I'm dreaming! I'm dreaming!" he repeated to himself. And he went on sleeping.

When he awoke the sky was clear; the loose window let in a cold, pure air. The Arab was asleep, hunched up under the blankets now, his mouth open, utterly relaxed. But when Daru shook him, he started dreadfully, staring at Daru with wild eyes as if he had never seen him and such a frightened expression that the schoolmaster stepped back. "Don't be afraid. It's me. You must eat." The Arab nodded his head and said yes. Calm had returned to his face, but his expression was vacant and listless.

The coffee was ready. They drank it seated together on the folding bed as they munched their pieces of the cake. Then Daru led the Arab under the shed and showed him the faucet where he washed. He went back into the room, folded the blankets and the bed, made his own bed and put the room in order. Then he went through the classroom and out onto the terrace. The sun was already rising in the blue sky; a soft, bright light was bathing the deserted plateau. On the ridge the snow was melting in spots. The stones were about to reappear. Crouched on the edge of the plateau, the schoolmaster looked at the deserted expanse. He thought of Balducci. He had hurt him, for he had sent him off in a way as if he didn't want to be associated with him. He could still hear the gendarme's farewell and, without knowing why, he felt strangely empty and vulnerable. At that moment, from the other side of the schoolhouse, the prisoner coughed. Daru listened to him almost despite himself and then, furious, threw a pebble that whistled through the air before sinking into the snow. That man's stupid crime revolted

him, but to hand him over was contrary to honor. Merely thinking of it made him smart with humiliation. And he cursed at one and the same time his own people who had sent him this Arab and the Arab, too, who had dared to kill and not managed to get away. Daru got up, walked in a circle on the terrace, waited motionless, and then went back into the schoolhouse.

The Arab, leaning over the cement floor of the shed, was washing his teeth with two fingers. Daru looked at him and said: "Come." He went back into the room ahead of the prisoner. He slipped a hunting jacket on over his sweater and put on walking shoes. Standing, he waited until the Arab had put on his *chèche* and sandals. They went into the classroom and the schoolmaster pointed to the exit, saying: "Go ahead." The fellow didn't budge. "I'm coming," said Daru. The Arab went out. Daru went back into the room and made a package of pieces of rusk, dates, and sugar. In the classroom, before going out, he hesitated a second in front of his desk, then crossed the threshold and locked the door. "That's the way," he said. He started toward the east, followed by the prisoner. But, a short distance from the schoolhouse, he thought he heard a slight sound behind them. He retraced his steps and examined the surroundings of the house; there was no one there. The Arab watched him without seeming to understand, "Come on," said Daru.

They walked for an hour and rested beside a sharp peak of limestone. The snow was melting faster and faster and the sun was drinking up the puddles at once, rapidly cleaning the plateau, which gradually dried and vibrated like the air itself. When they resumed walking, the ground rang under their feet. From time to time a bird rent the space in front of them with a joyful cry. Daru breathed in deeply the fresh morning light. He felt a sort of rapture before the vast familiar expanse, now almost entirely yellow under its dome of blue sky. They walked an hour more, descending toward the south. They reached a level height made up of crumbly rocks. From there on the plateau sloped down, eastward, toward a low plain where there were a few spindly trees and, to the south, toward outcroppings of rock that gave the landscape a chaotic look.

Daru surveyed the two directions. There was nothing but the sky on the horizon. Not a man could be seen. He turned toward the Arab, who was looking at him blankly. Daru held out the package to him. "Take it," he said. "There are dates, bread, and sugar. You can hold out for two days. Here are a thousand francs,

too." The Arab took the package and the money but kept his full hands at chest level as if he didn't know what to do with what was being given him. "Now look," the schoolmaster said as he pointed in the direction of the east, "there's the way to Tinguit. You have a two-hour walk. At Tinguit you'll find the administration and the police. They are expecting you." The Arab looked toward the east, still holding the package and the money against his chest. Daru took his elbow and turned him rather roughly toward the south. At the foot of the height on which they stood could be seen a faint path. "That's the trail across the plateau. In a day's walk from here you'll find pasturelands and the first nomads. They'll take you in and shelter you according to their law." The Arab had now turned toward Daru and a sort of panic was visible in his expression. "Listen," he said. Daru shook his head: "No, be quiet. Now I'm leaving you." He turned his back on him, took two long steps in the direction of the school, looked hesitantly at the motionless Arab, and started off again. For a few minutes he heard nothing but his own step resounding on the cold ground and did not turn his head. A moment later, however, he turned around. The Arab was still there on the edge of the hill, his arms hanging now, and he was looking at the schoolmaster. Daru felt something rise in his throat. But he swore with impatience, waved vaguely, and started off again. He had already gone some distance when he again stopped and looked. There was no longer anyone on the hill.

Daru hesitated. The sun was now rather high in the sky and was beginning to beat down on his head. The schoolmaster retraced his steps, at first somewhat uncertainly, then with decision. When he reached the little hill, he was bathed in sweat. He climbed it as fast as he could and stopped, out of breath, at the top. The rock fields to the south stood out sharply against the blue sky, but on the plain to the east a steamy heat was already rising. And in that slight haze, Daru, with heavy heart, made out the Arab walking slowly on the road to prison.

A little later, standing before the window of the classroom, the schoolmaster was watching the clear light bathing the whole surface of the plateau, but he hardly saw it. Behind him on the blackboard, among the winding French rivers, sprawled the clumsily chalked-up words he had just read: "You handed over our brother. You will pay for this." Daru looked at the sky, the plateau, and, beyond, the invisible lands stretching all the way to the sea. In this vast landscape he had loved so much, he was alone.

Lament for Ignacio Sánchez Mejías

Federico García Lorca

1. *Cogida and Death*

At five in the afternoon.
It was exactly five in the afternoon.
A boy brought the white sheet
at five in the afternoon.

A frail of lime ready prepared
at five in the afternoon.
The rest was death, and death alone
at five in the afternoon.

The wind carried away the cottonwool
at five in the afternoon.
And the oxide scattered crystal and nickel
at five in the afternoon.

Now the dove and the leopard wrestle
at five in the afternoon.
And a thigh with a desolate horn
at five in the afternoon.
The bass-string struck up
at five in the afternoon.
Arsenic bells and smoke
at five in the afternoon.
Groups of silence in the corners
at five in the afternoon.
And the bull alone with a high heart!
At five in the afternoon.
When the sweat of snow was coming
at five in the afternoon,
when the bull ring was covered in iodine
at five in the afternoon,
death laid eggs in the wound

at five in the afternoon.
At five in the afternoon.
Exactly at five o'clock in the afternoon.

A coffin on wheels is his bed
at five in the afternoon.
Bones and flutes resound in his ears
at five in the afternoon.
Now the bull was bellowing through his forehead
at five in the afternoon.
The room was iridescent with agony
at five in the afternoon.
In the distance the gangrene now comes
at five in the afternoon
Horn of the lily through green groins
at five in the afternoon.
The wounds were burning like suns
at five in the afternoon,
and the crowd was breaking the windows
at five in the afternoon.
At five in the afternoon.
Ah, that fatal five in the afternoon!
It was five by all the clocks!
It was five in the shade of the afternoon!

2. *The Spilled Blood*

I will not see it!

Tell the moon to come
for I do not want to see the blood
of Ignacio on the sand.

I will not see it!

The moon wide open.
Horse of still clouds,
and the grey bull ring of dreams
with willows in the barreras.

I will not see it!

Let my memory kindle!

Warn the jasmines
of such minute whiteness!

I will not see it!

The cow of the ancient world
passed her sad tongue
over a snout of blood
spilled on the sand,
and the bulls of Guisando,
partly death and partly stone,
bellowed like two centuries
sated with treading the earth.
No.
I do not want to see it!
I will not see it!

Ignacio goes up the tiers
with all his death on his shoulders.
He sought for the dawn
but the dawn was no more.
He seeks for his confident profile
and the dream bewilders him.
He sought for his beautiful body
and encountered his opened blood.
I will not see it!
I do not want to hear it spurt
each time with less strength:
that spurt that illuminates
the tiers of seats, and spills
over the corduroy and the leather
of a thirsty multitude.
Who shouts that I should come near!
Do not ask me to see it!

His eyes did not close
when he saw the horns near,
but the terrible mothers
lifted their heads.
And across the ranches,
an air of secret voices rose,
shouting to celestial bulls,
herdsmen of pale mist.

There was no prince in Seville
who could compare with him,
nor sword like his sword
nor heart so true.

Like a river of lions
was his marvellous strength,
and like a marble torso
his firm drawn moderation.
The air of Andalusian Rome
gilded his head
where his smile was a spikenard
of wit and intelligence.
What a great torero in the ring!
What a good peasant in the sierra!
How gentle with the sheaves!
How hard with the spurs!
How tender with the dew!
How dazzling in the fiesta!
How tremendous with the final
banderillas of darkness!

But now he sleeps without end.
Now the moss and the grass
open with sure fingers
the flower of his skull.
And now his blood comes out singing;
singing along marshes and meadows,
sliding on frozen horns,
faltering soulless in the mist,
stumbling over a thousand hoofs
like a long, dark, sad tongue,
to form a pool of agony
close to the starry Guadalquivir.
Oh, white wall of Spain!
Oh, black bull of sorrow!
Oh, hard blood of Ignacio!
Oh, nightingale of his veins!

No.
I will not see it!
No chalice can contain it,

no swallows can drink it,
no frost of light can cool it,
nor song nor deluge of white lilies,
no glass can cover it with silver.
No.
I will not see it!

3. *The Laid Out Body*

Stone is a forehead where dreams grieve
without curving waters and frozen cypresses.
Stone is a shoulder on which to bear Time
with trees formed of tears and ribbons and planets.

I have seen grey showers move towards the waves
raising their tender riddled arms,
to avoid being caught by the lying stone
which loosens their limbs without soaking the blood.

For stone gathers seed and clouds,
skeleton larks and wolves of penumbra:
but yields not sounds nor crystals nor fire,
only bull rings and bull rings and more bull rings without
    walls.

Now, Ignacio the well born lies on the stone.
All is finished. What is happening? Contemplate his face:
death has covered him with pale sulphur
and has placed on him the head of a dark minotaur.

All is finished. The rain penetrates his mouth.
The air, as if mad, leaves his sunken chest,
and Love, soaked through with tears of snow,
warms itself on the peak of the herd.

What are they saying? A stenching silence settles down.
We are here with a body laid out which fades away,
with a pure shape which had nightingales
and we see it being filled with depthless holes.

Who creases the shroud? What he says is not true!
Nobody sings here, nobody weeps in the corner,

nobody pricks the spurs, nor terrifies the serpent.
Here I want nothing else but the round eyes
to see this body without a chance of rest.

Here I want to see those men of hard voice.
Those that break horses and dominate rivers;
those men of sonorous skeleton who sing
with a mouth full of sun and flint.

Here I want to see them. Before the stone.
Before this body with broken reins.
I want to know from them the way out
for this captain strapped down by death.

I want them to show me a lament like a river
which will have sweet mists and deep shores,
to take the body of Ignacio where it loses itself
without hearing the double panting of the bulls.

Loses itself in the round bull ring of the moon
which feigns in its youth a sad quiet bull:
loses itself in the night without song of fishes
and in the white thicket of frozen smoke.

I don't want them to cover his face with handkerchiefs
that he may get used to the death he carries.
Go, Ignacio; feel not the hot bellowing.
Sleep, fly, rest: even the sea dies!

4. *Absent Soul*

The bull does not know you, nor the fig tree,
nor the horses, nor the ants in your own house.
The child and the afternoon do not know you
because you have died for ever.

The back of the stone does not know you,
nor the black satin in which you crumble.
Your silent memory does not know you
because you have died for ever.

The autumn will come with small white snails,
misty grapes and with clustered hills,
but no one will look into your eyes
because you have died for ever.

Because you have died for ever,
like all the dead of the Earth,
like all the dead who are forgotten
in a heap of lifeless dogs.

Nobody knows you. No. But I sing of you.
For posterity I sing of your profile and grace.
Of the signal maturity of your understanding.
Of your appetite for death and the taste of its mouth.
Of the sadness of your once valiant gaiety.

It will be a long time, if ever, before there is born
an Andalusian so true, so rich in adventure.
I sing of his elegance with words that groan,
and I remember a sad breeze through the olive trees.

A Gazelle: *from* Out of Africa

Isak Dinesen

LULU came to my house from the woods as Kamante had come to it from the plains.

To the east of my farm lay the Ngong Forest Reserve, which then was nearly all virgin forest. To my mind it was a sad thing when the old forest was cut down, and eucalyptus and grevillea planted in its place; it might have made a unique pleasure ground and park for Nairobi.

An African native forest is a mysterious region. You ride into the depths of an old tapestry, in places faded and in others darkened with age, but marvelously rich in green shades. You cannot see the sky at all in there, but the sunlight plays in many strange ways, falling through the foliage. The gray fungus, like long drooping beards, on the trees, and the creepers hanging down everywhere, give a secretive, recondite air to the native forest. I used to ride here with Farah on Sundays, when there was nothing to do on the farm, up and down the slopes, and across the little winding forest streams. The air in the forest was cool like water, and filled with the scent of plants, and in the beginning of the long rains when the creepers flowered, you rode through sphere after sphere of fragrance. One kind of African Daphne of the woods, which flowers with a small cream-colored sticky blossom, had an overwhelming sweet perfume, like lilac, and wild lily of the valley. Here and there, hollow tree stems were hung up in ropes of hide on a branch; the Kikuyu hung them there to make the bees build in them, and to get honey. Once as we turned a corner in the forest, we saw a leopard sitting on the road, a tapestry animal.

Here, high above the ground, lived a garrulous restless nation, the little gray monkeys. Where a pack of monkeys had travelled over the road, the smell of them lingered for a long time in the air, a dry and stale, mousy smell. As you rode on you would suddenly hear the rush and whizz over your head, as the colony passed along on its own ways. If you kept still in the same place for some time you might catch sight of one of the monkeys sitting immovable in a tree, and, a little after, discover that the whole forest round you was alive with his family, placed like fruits on the branches, grey or dark figures according to how the sunlight fell on them, all with their long tails hanging down be-

hind them. They gave out a peculiar sound, like a smacking kiss with a little cough to follow it; if from the ground you imitated it, you saw the monkeys turn their heads from one side to the other in an affected manner, but if you made a sudden movement they were all off in a second, and you could follow the decreasing swash as they clove the treetops, and disappeared in the wood like a shoal of fishes in the waves.

In the Ngong Forest I have also seen, on a narrow path through thick growth, in the middle of a very hot day, the Giant Forest Hog, a rare person to meet. He came suddenly past me, with his wife and three young pigs, at a great speed, the whole family looking like uniform, bigger and smaller figures cut out in dark paper, against the sunlit green behind them. It was a glorious sight, like a reflection in a forest pool, like a thing that had happened a thousand years ago.

Lulu was a young antelope of the bushbuck tribe, which is perhaps the prettiest of all the African antelopes. They are a little bigger than the fallow deer; they live in the woods, or in the bush, and are shy and fugitive, so that they are not seen as often as the antelopes of the plains. But the Ngong Hills, and the surrounding country, were good places for bushbuck, and if you had your camp in the hills, and were out hunting in the early morning, or at sunset, you would see them come out of the bush into the glades, and as the rays of the sun fell upon them their coats shone red as copper. The male has a pair of delicately turned horns.

Lulu became a member of my household in this way:

I drove one morning from the farm to Nairobi. My mill on the farm had burnt down a short time before, and I had had to drive into town many times to get the insurance settled and paid out; in this early morning I had my head filled with figures and estimates. As I came driving along the Ngong Road a little group of Kikuyu children shouted to me from the roadside, and I saw that they were holding a very small bushbuck up for me to see. I knew that they would have found the fawn in the bush, and that now they wanted to sell it to me, but I was late for an appointment in Nairobi, and I had no thought for this sort of thing, so I drove on.

When I was coming back in the evening and was driving past the same place, there was again a great shout from the side of the road and the small party was still there, a little tired and disappointed, for they may have tried to sell the fawn to other people passing by in the course of the day, but keen now to get the deal

through before the sun was down, and they held up the fawn high to tempt me. But I had had a long day in town, and some adversity about the insurance, so that I did not care to stop or talk, and I just drove on past them. I did not even think of them when I was back in my house, and dined and went to bed.

The moment that I had fallen asleep I was woken up again by a great feeling of terror. The picture of the boys and the small buck, which had now collected and taken shape, stood out before me, clearly, as if it had been painted, and I sat up in bed as appalled as if someone had been trying to choke me. What, I thought, would become of the fawn in the hands of the captors who had stood with it in the heat of the long day, and had held it up by its joined legs? It was surely too young to eat on its own. I myself had driven past it twice on the same day, like the priest and the Levite in one, and had given no thought to it, and now, at this moment, where was it? I got up in a real panic and woke up all my houseboys. I told them that the fawn must be found and brought me in the morning, or they would all of them get their dismissal from my service. They were immediately up to the idea. Two of my boys had been in the car with me the same day, and had not shown the slightest interest in the children or the fawn; now they came forward, and gave the others a long list of details of the place and the hour and of the family of the boys. It was a moonlight night; my people all took off and spread in the landscape in a lively discussion of the situation; I heard them expatiating on the fact that they were all to be dismissed in case the bushbuck were not found.

Early next morning when Farah brought me in my tea, Juma came in with him and carried the fawn in his arms. It was a female, and we named her Lulu, which I was told was the Swahili word for a pearl.

Lulu by that time was only as big as a cat, with large quiet purple eyes. She had such delicate legs that you feared they would not bear being folded up and unfolded again, as she lay down and rose up. Her ears were smooth as silk and exceedingly expressive. Her nose was as black as a truffle. Her diminutive hoofs gave her all the air of a young Chinese lady of the old school, with laced feet. It was a rare experience to hold such a perfect thing in your hands.

Lulu soon adapted herself to the house and its inhabitants and behaved as if she were at home. During the first weeks the polished floors in the rooms were a problem in her life, and

when she got outside the carpets her legs went away from her to all four sides; it looked catastrophic but she did not let it worry her much and in the end she learnt to walk on the bare floors with a sound like a succession of little angry finger taps. She was extraordinarily neat in all her habits. She was headstrong already as a child, but when I stopped her from doing the things she wanted to do, she behaved as if she said: Anything rather than a scene.

Kamante brought her up on a sucking bottle, and he also shut her up at night, for we had to be careful of her as the leopards were up round the house after nightfall. So she held to him and followed him about. From time to time when he did not do what she wanted, she gave his thin legs a hard butt with her young head, and she was so pretty that you could not help, when you looked upon the two together, seeing them as a new paradoxical illustration to the tale of the Beauty and the Beast. On the strength of this great beauty and gracefulness, Lulu obtained for herself a commanding position in the house, and was treated with respect by all.

In Africa I never had dogs of any other breed than the Scotch deerhound. There is no more noble or gracious kind of dog. They must have lived for many centuries with men to understand and fall in with our life and its conditions the way they do. You will also find them in old paintings and tapestries, and they have in themselves a tendency to change, by their looks and manners, their surroundings into tapestry; they bring with them a feudal atmosphere.

The first of my tribe of deerhounds, who was named Dusk, had been given to me as a wedding present, and had come out with me when I began my life in Africa, on "The Mayflower," so to say. He was a gallant, generous character. He accompanied me when, during the first months of the war, I did transport for the government, with ox wagons in the Masai Reserve. But a couple of years later he was killed by zebra. By the time that Lulu came to live in my house I had two of his sons there.

The Scotch deerhound went well with African scenery and the African native. It may be due to the altitude—the highland melody in all three—for he did not look so harmonious at sea level in Mombasa. It was as if the great, spare landscape, with the plains, hills and rivers, was not complete until the deerhounds were also in it. All the deerhounds were great hunters and had more nose than the greyhounds, but they hunted by

sight and it was a highly wonderful thing to see two of them working together. I took them with me when I was out riding in the game reserve, which I was not allowed to do, and there they would spread the herds of zebra and wildebeest over the plain, as if it were all the stars of heaven running wild over the sky. But when I was out in the Masai Reserve shooting I never lost a wounded head of game, if I had the deerhounds with me.

They looked well in the native forests too, dark gray in the sombre green shades. One of them, in here, all by himself, killed a big old male baboon, and in the fight had his nose bitten straight through, which spoilt his noble profile but by everybody on the farm was considered an honorable scar, for the baboons are destructive beasts and the Natives detest them.

The deerhounds were very wise, and knew who amongst my houseboys were Mohammedans, and not allowed to touch dogs.

During my first years in Africa I had a Somali gun bearer named Ismail, who died while I was still out there. He was one of the old-time gun bearers and there are no such people now. He had been brought up by the great old big-game hunters of the beginning of the century, when all Africa was a real deer park. His acquaintance with civilization was entirely of the hunting fields, and he spoke an English of the hunting world, so that he would talk of my big and my young rifle. After Ismail had gone back to Somaliland, I had a letter from him which was addressed to _Lioness Blixen,_ and opened: _Honorable Lioness._ Ismail was a strict Mohammedan, and would not for the life of him touch a dog, which caused him much worry in his profession. But he made an exception with Dusk and never minded my taking him with us in the mule trap; he would even let Dusk sleep in his tent. For Dusk, he said, would know a Mohammedan when he saw him, and would never touch him. Indeed, Ismail assured me, Dusk could see at once who was a sincere Mohammedan at heart. He once said to me: "I know now that the Dusk is of the same tribe as you yourself. He laughs at the people."

Now my dogs understood Lulu's power and position in the house. The arrogance of the great hunters was like water with her. She pushed them away from the milk bowl and from their favorite places in front of the fire. I had tied a small bell on a rein round Lulu's neck, and there came a time when the dogs, when they heard the jingle of it approaching through the rooms, would get up resignedly from their warm beds by the fireplace, and go

and lie down in some other part of the room. Still nobody could be of a gentler demeanor than Lulu was when she came and lay down, in the manner of a perfect lady who demurely gathers her skirts about her and will be in no one's way. She drank the milk with a polite, pernickety mien, as if she had been pressed by an overkind hostess. She insisted on being scratched behind the ears, in a pretty forbearing way, like a young wife who pertly permits her husband a caress.

When Lulu grew up and stood in the flower of her young loveliness she was a slim delicately rounded doe, from her nose to her toes unbelievably beautiful. She looked like a minutely painted illustration to Heine's song of the wise and gentle gazelles by the flow of the river Ganges.

But Lulu was not really gentle; she had the so called devil in her. She had, to the highest degree, the feminine trait of appearing to be exclusively on the defensive, concentrated on guarding the integrity of her being, when she was really, with every force in her, bent upon the offensive. Against whom? Against the whole world. Her moods grew beyond control or computation, and she would go for my horse, if he displeased her. I remembered old Hagenbeck in Hamburg, who had said that of all animal races, the carnivora included, the deer are the least to be relied on, and that you may trust a leopard, but if you trust a young stag, sooner or later he falls upon you in the rear.

Lulu was the pride of the house even when she behaved like a real shameless young coquette; but we did not make her happy. Sometimes she walked away from the house for hours, or for a whole afternoon. Sometimes when the spirit came upon her and her discontent with her surroundings reached a climax, she would perform, for the satisfaction of her own heart, on the lawn in front of the house, a war dance, which looked like a brief zigzagged prayer to Satan.

"Oh Lulu," I thought, "I know that you are marvelously strong and that you can leap higher than your own height. You are furious with us now, you wish that we were all dead, and indeed we should be so if you could be bothered to kill us. But the trouble is not as you think now, that we have put up obstacles too high for you to jump, and how could we possibly do that, you great leaper? It is that we have put up no obstacles at all. The great strength is in you, Lulu, and the obstacles are within you as well, and the thing is, that the fullness of time has not yet come."

One evening Lulu did not come home and we looked out for her in vain for a week. This was a hard blow to us all. A clear note had gone out of the house and it seemed no better than other houses. I thought of the leopards by the river and one evening I talked about them to Kamante.

As usual he waited some time before he answered, to digest my lack of insight. It was not till a few days later that he approached me upon the matter. "You believe that Lulu is dead, Msabu," he said.

I did not like to say so straight out, but I told him I was wondering why she did not come back.

"Lulu," said Kamante, "is not dead. But she is married."

This was pleasant, surprising news, and I asked him how he knew of it.

"Oh yes," he said, "she is married. She lives in the forest with her *bwana*,"—her husband, or master. "But she has not forgotten the people; most mornings she is coming back to the house. I lay out crushed maize to her at the back of the kitchen, then just before the sun comes up, she walks round there from the woods and eats it. Her husband is with her, but he is afraid of the people because he has never known them. He stands below the big white tree by the other side of the lawn. But up to the houses he dares not come."

I told Kamante to come and fetch me when he next saw Lulu. A few days later before sunrise he came and called me out.

It was a lovely morning. The last stars withdrew while we were waiting, the sky was clear and serene but the world in which we walked was sombre still, and profoundly silent. The grass was wet; down by the trees where the ground sloped it gleamed with the dew like dim silver. The air of the morning was cold, it had that twinge in it which in northern countries means that the frost is not far away. However often you make the experience, I thought, it is still impossible to believe, in this coolness and shade, that the heat of the sun and the glare of the sky, in a few hours' time, will be hard to bear. The gray mist lay upon the hills, strangely taking shape from them; it would be bitterly cold on the buffalo if they were about there now, grazing on the hillside, as in a cloud.

The great vault over our heads was gradually filled with clarity like a glass with wine. Suddenly, gently, the summits of the hills caught the first sunlight and blushed. And slowly, as the earth leaned toward the sun, the grassy slopes at the foot of the

mountain turned a delicate gold, and the Masai woods lower down. And now the tops of the tall trees in the forest, on our side of the river, blushed like copper. This was the hour for the flight of the big purple wood pigeons which roosted by the other side of the river and came over to feed on the Cape chestnuts in my forest. They were here only for a short season in the year. The birds came surprisingly fast, like a cavalry attack of the air. For this reason the morning pigeon shooting on the farm was popular with my friends in Nairobi; to be out by the house in time, just as the sun rose, they used to come out so early that they rounded my drive with the lamps of their cars still lighted.

Standing like this in the limpid shadow, looking up toward the golden heights and the clear sky, you would get the feeling that you were in reality walking along the bottom of the sea, with the currents running by you, and were gazing up toward the surface of the ocean.

A bird began to sing, and then I heard, a little way off in the forest, the tinkling of a bell. Yes, it was a joy, Lulu was back, and about in her old places! It came nearer, I could follow her movements by its rhythm; she was walking, stopping, walking on again. A turning round one of the boys' huts brought her upon us. It suddenly became an unusual and amusing thing to see a bushbuck so close to the house. She stood immovable now, she seemed to be prepared for the sight of Kamante, but not for that of me. But she did not make off, she looked at me without fear and without any remembrance of our skirmishes of the past or of her own ingratitude in running away without warning.

Lulu of the woods was a superior, independent being, a change of heart had come upon her, she was in possession. If I had happened to have known a young princess in exile, and while she was still a pretender to the throne, and had met her again in her full queenly estate after she had come into her rights, our meeting would have had the same character. Lulu showed no more meanness of heart than King Louis Philippe did, when he declared that the King of France did not remember the grudges of the Duke of Orléans. She was now the complete Lulu. The spirit of offensive had gone from her; for whom, and why, should she attack? She was standing quietly on her divine rights. She remembered me enough to feel that I was nothing to be afraid of. For a minute she gazed at me; her purple smoky eyes were absolutely without expression and did not wink, and I

remembered that the gods or goddesses never wink, and felt that I was face to face with the ox-eyed Hera. She lightly nipped a leaf of grass as she passed me, made one pretty little leap, and walked on to the back of the kitchen, where Kamante had spread maize on the ground.

Kamante touched my arm with one finger and then pointed it toward the woods. As I followed the direction, I saw, under a tall Cape chestnut tree, a male bushbuck, a small tawny silhouette at the outskirt of the forest, with a fine pair of horns, immovable like a tree stem. Kamante observed him for some time, and then laughed.

"Look here now," he said, "Lulu has explained to her husband that there is nothing up by the houses to be afraid of, but all the same he dares not come. Every morning he thinks that today he will come all the way, but, when he sees the house and the people, he gets a cold stone in the stomach"—this is a common thing in the native world, and often gets in the way of the work on the farm—"and then he stops by the tree."

For a long time Lulu came to the house in the early mornings. Her clear bell announced that the sun was up on the hills; I used to lie in bed, and wait for it. Sometimes she stayed away for a week or two, and we missed her and began to talk of the people who went to shoot in the hills. But then again my houseboys announced: "Lulu is here," as if it had been the married daughter of the house on a visit. A few times more I also saw the bushbuck's silhouette amongst the trees, but Kamante had been right, and he never collected enough courage to come all the way to the house.

One day, as I came back from Nairobi, Kamante was keeping watch for me outside the kitchen door, and stepped forward, much excited, to tell me that Lulu had been to the farm the same day and had had her Toto—her baby—with her. Some days after, I myself had the honor to meet her amongst the boys' huts, much on the alert and not to be trifled with, with a very small fawn at her heels, as delicately tardive in his movements as Lulu herself had been when we first knew her. This was just after the long rains, and, during those summer months, Lulu was to be found near the houses, in the afternoon, as well as at daybreak. She would even be round there at midday, keeping in the shadow of the huts.

Lulu's fawn was not afraid of the dogs, and would let them sniff him all over, but he could not get used to the natives or to

me, and if we ever tried to get hold of him, the mother and the child were off.

Lulu herself would never, after her first long absence from the house, come so near to any of us that we could touch her. In other ways she was friendly, she understood that we wanted to look at her fawn, and she would take a piece of sugarcane from an outstretched hand. She walked up to the open dining-room door, and gazed thoughtfully into the twilight of the rooms, but she never again crossed the threshold. She had by this time lost her bell, and came and went away in silence.

My houseboys suggested that I should let them catch Lulu's fawn, and keep him as we had once kept Lulu. But I thought it would make a boorish return to Lulu's elegant confidence in us.

It also seemed to me that the free union between my house and the antelope was a rare, honorable thing. Lulu came in from the wild world to show that we were on good terms with it, and she made my house one with the African landscape, so that nobody could tell where the one stopped and the other began. Lulu knew the place of the Giant Forest Hog's lair and had seen the rhino. In Africa there is a cuckoo which sings in the middle of the hot days in the midst of the forest, like the sonorous heartbeat of the world; I had never had the luck to see her, neither had anyone that I knew, for nobody could tell me how she looked. But Lulu had perhaps walked on a narrow green deer path just under the branch on which the cuckoo was sitting. I was then reading a book about the old great Empress of China, and of how after the birth of her son, young Yahanola came on a visit to her old home; she set forth from the Forbidden City in her golden, green-hung palanquin. My house, I thought, was now like the house of the young Empress's father and mother.

The two antelopes, the big and the small, were round by my house all that summer; sometimes there was an interval of a fortnight, or three weeks, between their visits, but at other times we saw them every day. In the beginning of the next rainy season my houseboys told me that Lulu had come back with a new fawn. I did not see the fawn myself, for by this time they did not come up quite close to the house, but later I saw three bushbucks together in the forest.

The league between Lulu and her family and my house lasted for many years. The bushbucks were often in the neighborhood of the house, they came out of the woods and went back again as if my grounds were a province of the wild country. They came

mostly just before sunset, and first moved in amongst the trees like delicate dark silhouettes on the dark trees, but when they stepped out to graze on the lawn in the light of the afternoon sun their coats shone like copper. One of them was Lulu, for she came up near to the house, and walked about sedately, pricking her ears when a car arrived, or when we opened a window; and the dogs would know her. She became darker in color with age. Once I came driving up in front of my house with a friend and found three bushbucks on the terrace there, round the salt that was laid out for my cows.

It was a curious thing that apart from the first big bushbuck, Lulu's *bwana,* who had stood under the Cape chestnut with his head up, no male bushbuck was amongst the antelopes that came to my house. It seemed that we had to do with a forest matriarchy.

The hunters and naturalists of the colony took an interest in my bushbucks, and the game warden drove out to the farm to see them, and did see them there. A correspondent wrote about them in the *East African Standard.*

The years in which Lulu and her people came round to my house were the happiest of my life in Africa. For that reason, I came to look upon my acquaintance with the forest antelopes as a great boon, and a token of friendship from Africa. All the country was in it, good omens, old covenants, a song:

"Make haste, my beloved and be thou like to a roe or to a young hart upon the mountain of spices."

During my last years in Africa I saw less and less of Lulu and her family. Within the year before I went away I do not think that they ever came. Things had changed; south of my farm, land had been given out to farmers and the forest had been cleared here, and houses built. Tractors were heaving up and down where the glades had been. Many of the new settlers were keen sportsmen and the rifles sang in the landscape. I believe that the game withdrew to the West and went into the woods of the Masai Reserve.

I do not know how long an antelope lives; probably Lulu has died a long time ago.

Often, very often, in the quiet hours of daybreak, I have dreamed that I have heard Lulu's clear bell, and in my sleep my heart has run full of joy, I have woken up expecting something very strange and sweet to happen, just now, in a moment.

When I have then lain and thought of Lulu, I have wondered if in her life in the woods she ever dreamed of the bell. Would there pass in her mind, like shadows upon water, pictures of people and dogs?

If I know a song of Africa, I thought—of the Giraffe, and the African new moon lying on her back, of the ploughs in the fields, and the sweaty faces of the coffee pickers—does Africa know a song of me? Would the air over the plain quiver with a color that I had on, or the children invent a game in which my name was, or the full moon throw a shadow over the gravel of the drive that was like me, or would the eagles of Ngong look out for me?

The Pearl

Yukio Mishima

DECEMBER 10 was Mrs. Sasaki's birthday, but since it was Mrs. Sasaki's wish to celebrate the occasion with the minimum of fuss, she had invited to her house for afternoon tea only her closest friends. Assembled were Mesdames Yamamoto, Matsumura, Azuma, and Kasuga—all four being forty-three years of age, exact contemporaries of their hostess.

These ladies were thus members, as it were, of a Keep-Our-Ages-Secret Society and could be trusted implicitly not to divulge to outsiders the number of candles on today's cake. In inviting to her birthday party only guests of this nature, Mrs. Sasaki was showing her customary prudence.

On this occasion Mrs. Sasaki wore a pearl ring. Diamonds at an all-female gathering had not seemed in the best of taste. Furthermore, pearls better matched the color of the dress she was wearing on this particular day.

Shortly after the party had begun, Mrs. Sasaki was moving across for one last inspection of the cake when the pearl in her ring, already a little loose, finally fell from its socket. It seemed a most inauspicious event for this happy occasion, but it would have been no less embarrassing to have everyone aware of the misfortune, so Mrs. Sasaki simply left the pearl close by the rim of the large cake dish and resolved to do something about it later. Around the cake were set out the plates, forks, and paper napkins for herself and the four guests. It now occurred to Mrs. Sasaki that she had no wish to be seen wearing a ring with no stone while cutting this cake, and accordingly she removed the ring from her finger and very deftly, without turning around, slipped it into a recess in the wall behind her back.

Amid the general excitement of the exchange of gossip, and Mrs. Sasaki's surprise and pleasure at the thoughtful presents brought by her guests, the matter of the pearl was very quickly forgotten. Before long it was time for the customary ceremony of lighting and extinguishing the candles on the cake. Everyone crowded excitedly about the table, lending a hand in the not untroublesome task of lighting forty-three candles.

Mrs. Sasaki, with her limited lung capacity, could hardly be expected to blow out all that number at one puff, and her appearance

of utter helplessness gave rise to a great deal of hilarious comment.

The procedure followed in serving the cake was that, after the first bold cut, Mrs. Sasaki carved for each guest individually a slice of whatever thickness was requested and transferred this to a small plate, which the guest then carried back with her to her own seat. With everyone stretching out hands at the same time, the crush and confusion around the table was considerable.

On top of the cake was a floral design executed in pink icing and liberally interspersed with small silver balls. These were silver-painted crystals of sugar—a common enough decoration on birthday cakes. In the struggle to secure helpings, moreover, flakes of icing, crumbs of cake, and a number of these silver balls came to be scattered all over the white tablecloth. Some of the guests gathered these stray particles between their fingers and put them on their plates. Others popped them straight into their mouths.

In time all returned to their seats and ate their portions of cake at their leisure, laughing. It was not a homemade cake, having been ordered by Mrs. Sasaki from a certain high-class confectioner's, but the guests were unanimous in praising its excellence.

Mrs. Sasaki was bathed in happiness. But suddenly, with a tinge of anxiety, she recalled the pearl she had abandoned on the table, and rising from her chair as casually as she could, she moved across to look for it. At the spot where she was sure she had left it, the pearl was no longer to be seen.

Mrs. Sasaki abhorred losing things. At once and without thinking, right in the middle of the party, she became wholly engrossed in her search, and the tension in her manner was so obvious that it attracted everyone's attention.

"Is there something the matter?" someone asked.

"No, not at all, just a moment. . . ."

Mrs. Sasaki's reply was ambiguous, but before she had time to decide to return to her chair, first one, then another, and finally every one of her guests had risen and was turning back the tablecloth or groping about on the floor.

Mrs. Azuma, seeing this commotion, felt that the whole thing was just too deplorable for words. She was incensed at a hostess who could create such an impossible situation over the loss of a solitary pearl.

Mrs. Azuma resolved to offer herself as a sacrifice and to save the day. With a heroic smile she declared: "That's it then! It must have been a pearl I ate just now! A silver ball dropped on

the tablecloth when I was given my cake, and I just picked it up and swallowed it without thinking. It *did* seem to stick in my throat a little. Had it been a diamond, now, I would naturally return it—by an operation, if necessary—but as it's a pearl, I must simply beg your forgiveness."

This announcement at once resolved the company's anxieties, and it was felt, above all, that it had saved the hostess from an embarrassing predicament. No one made any attempt to investigate the truth or falsity of Mrs. Azuma's confession. Mrs. Sasaki took one of the remaining silver balls and put it in her mouth.

"Mm," she said. "Certainly tastes like a pearl, this one!"

Thus, this small incident, too, was cast into the crucible of good-humored teasing, and there—amid general laughter—it melted away.

When the party was over, Mrs. Azuma drove off in her two-seater sportscar, taking with her in the other seat her close friend and neighbor Mrs. Kasuga. Before two minutes had passed, Mrs. Azuma said, "Own up! It was you who swallowed the pearl, wasn't it? I covered up for you and took the blame on myself."

This unceremonious manner of speaking concealed deep affection, but however friendly the intention may have been, to Mrs. Kasuga a wrongful accusation was a wrongful accusation. She had no recollection whatsoever of having swallowed a pearl in mistake for a sugar ball. She was—as Mrs. Azuma too must surely know—fastidious in her eating habits, and if she so much as detected a single hair in her food, whatever she happened to be eating at the time immediately stuck in her gullet.

"Oh, really now!" protested the timid Mrs. Kasuga in a small voice, her eyes studying Mrs. Azuma's face in some puzzlement. "I just couldn't do a thing like that!"

"It's no good pretending. The moment I saw that green look on your face , I knew."

The little disturbance at the party had seemed closed by Mrs. Azuma's frank confession, but even now it had left behind it this strange awkwardness. Mrs. Kasuga, wondering how best to demonstrate her innocence, was at the same time seized by the fantasy that a solitary pearl was lodged somewhere in her intestines. It was unlikely, of course, that she should mistakenly swallow a pearl for a sugar ball, but in all that confusion of talk and laughter, one had to admit that it was at least a possibility. Though she thought back over the events of the party again and

again, no moment in which she might have inserted a pearl into her mouth came to mind—but after all, if it was an unconscious act, one would not expect to remember it.

Mrs. Kasuga blushed deeply as her imagination chanced upon one further aspect of the matter. It had occurred to her that when one accepted a pearl into one's system, it almost certainly—its luster a trifle dimmed, perhaps, by gastric juices—reemerged intact within a day or two.

And with this thought the design of Mrs. Azuma, too, seemed to have become transparently clear. Undoubtedly Mrs. Azuma had viewed this same prospect with embarrassment and shame and had therefore cast her responsibility onto another, making it appear that she had considerately taken the blame to protect a friend.

Meanwhile, Mrs. Yamamoto and Mrs. Matsumura, whose homes lay in a similar direction, were returning together in a taxi. Soon after the taxi had started, Mrs. Matsumura opened her handbag to make a few adjustments to her make-up. She remembered that she had done nothing to her face since all that commotion at the party.

As she was removing the powder compact, her attention was caught by a sudden dull gleam as something tumbled to the bottom of the bag. Groping about with the tips of her fingers, Mrs. Matsumura retrieved the object and saw to her amazement that it was a pearl.

Mrs. Matsumura stifled an exclamation of surprise. Recently her relationship with Mrs. Yamamoto had been far from cordial, and she had no wish to share with that lady a discovery with such awkward implications for herself.

Fortunately, Mrs. Yamamoto was gazing out the window and did not appear to have noticed her companion's momentary start of surprise.

Caught off balance by this sudden turn of events, Mrs. Matsumura did not pause to consider how the pearl had found its way into her bag but immediately became a prisoner of her own private brand of school-captain morality. It was unlikely—she thought—that she would do a thing like this, even in a moment of abstraction. But since, by some chance, the object had found its way into her handbag, the proper course was to return it at once. If she failed to do so, it would weigh heavily upon her conscience. The fact that it was a pearl, too—an article you could

call neither all that expensive nor yet all that cheap—only made her position more ambiguous.

At any rate, she was determined that her companion, Mrs. Yamamoto, should know nothing of this incomprehensible development—especially when the affair had been so nicely rounded off, thanks to the selflessness of Mrs. Azuma. Mrs. Matsumura felt she could remain in the taxi not a moment longer, and on the pretext of remembering a promise to visit a sick relative on her way back, she made the driver set her down at once, in the middle of a quiet residential district.

Mrs. Yamamoto, left alone in the taxi, was a little surprised that her practical joke should have moved Mrs. Matsumura to such abrupt action. Having watched Mrs. Matsumura's reflection in the window just now, she had clearly seen her draw the pearl from her bag.

At the party Mrs. Yamamoto had been the very first to receive a slice of cake. Adding to her plate a silver ball which had spilled onto the table, she had returned to her seat—again before any of the others—and there had noticed that the silver ball was a pearl. At this discovery she had at once conceived a malicious plan. While all the others were preoccupied with the cake, she had quickly slipped the pearl into the handbag left on the next chair by that insufferable hypocrite Mrs. Matsumura.

Stranded in the middle of a residential district where there was little prospect of a taxi, Mrs. Matsumura fretfully gave her mind to a number of reflections on her position.

First, no matter how necessary it might be for the relief of her own conscience, it would be a shame, indeed, when people had gone to such lengths to settle the affair satisfactorily, to go and stir up things all over again; and it would be even worse if in the process—because of the inexplicable nature of the circumstances—she were to direct unjust suspicions upon herself.

Secondly—notwithstanding these considerations—if she did not make haste to return the pearl now, she would forfeit her opportunity forever. Left till tomorrow (at the thought Mrs. Matsumura blushed), the returned pearl would be an object of rather disgusting speculation and doubt. Concerning this possibility, Mrs. Azuma herself had dropped a hint.

It was at this point that there occurred to Mrs. Matsumura, greatly to her joy, a master scheme which would both salve her conscience and at the same time involve no risk of exposing her character to any unjust suspicion. Quickening her step, she

emerged at length onto a comparatively busy thoroughfare, where she hailed a taxi and told the driver to take her quickly to a certain celebrated pearl shop on the Ginza. There she took the pearl from her bag and showed it to the attendant, asking to see a pearl of slightly larger size and clearly superior quality. Having made her purchase, she proceeded once more, by taxi, to Mrs. Sasaki's house.

Mrs. Matsumura's plan was to present this newly purchased pearl to Mrs. Sasaki, saying she had found it in her jacket pocket. Mrs. Sasaki would accept it and later attempt to fit it into the ring. However, being a pearl of a different size, it would not fit into the ring, and Mrs. Sasaki—puzzled—would try to return it to Mrs. Matsumura, but Mrs. Matsumura would refuse to have it returned. Thereupon Mrs. Sasaki would have no choice but to reflect as follows: The woman has behaved in this way in order to protect someone else. Such being the case, it is perhaps safest simply to accept the pearl and forget the matter. Mrs. Matsumura has doubtless observed one of the three ladies in the act of stealing the pearl. But at least, of my four guests, I can now be sure that Mrs. Matsumura, if no one else, is completely without guilt. Whoever heard of a thief stealing something and then replacing it with a similar article of greater value?

By this device Mrs. Matsumura proposed to escape forever the infamy of suspicion and equally—by a small outlay of cash—the pricks of an uneasy conscience.

To return to the other ladies. After reaching home, Mrs. Kasuga continued to feel painfully upset by Mrs. Azuma's cruel teasing. To clear herself of even a ridiculous charge like this— she knew—she must act before tomorrow or it would be too late. That is to say, in order to offer positive proof that she had not eaten the pearl, it was above all necessary for the pearl itself to be somehow produced. And, briefly, if she could show the pearl to Mrs. Azuma immediately, her innocence on the gastronomic count (if not on any other) would be firmly established. But if she waited until tomorrow, even though she managed to produce the pearl, the shameful and hardly mentionable suspicion would inevitably have intervened.

The normally timid Mrs. Kasuga, inspired with the courage of impetuous action, burst from the house to which she had so recently returned, sped to a pearl shop in the Ginza, and selected and bought a pearl which, to her eye, seemed of roughly the same

size as those silver balls on the cake. She then telephoned Mrs. Azuma. On returning home, she explained, she had discovered in the folds of the bow of her sash the pearl which Mrs. Sasaki had lost, but since she felt too ashamed to return it by herself, she wondered if Mrs. Azuma would be so kind as to go with her, as soon as possible. Inwardly Mrs. Azuma considered the story a little unlikely, but since it was the request of a good friend, she agreed to go.

Mrs. Sasaki accepted the pearl brought to her by Mrs. Matsumura and, puzzled at its failure to fit the ring, fell obligingly into that very train of thought for which Mrs. Matsumura had prayed; but it was a surprise to her when Mrs. Kasuga arrived about an hour later, accompanied by Mrs. Azuma, and returned another pearl.

Mrs. Sasaki hovered perilously on the brink of discussing Mrs. Matsumura's prior visit but checked herself at the last moment and accepted the second pearl as unconcernedly as she could. She felt sure that this one at any rate would fit, and as soon as the two visitors had taken their leave, she hurried to try it in the ring. But it was too small and wobbled loosely in the socket. At this discovery Mrs. Sasaki was not so much surprised as dumbfounded.

On the way back in the car, both ladies found it impossible to guess what the other might be thinking, and though normally relaxed and loquacious in each other's company, they now lapsed into a long silence.

Mrs. Azuma, who believed she could do nothing without her own full knowledge, knew for certain that she had not swallowed the pearl herself. It was simply to save everyone from embarrassment that she had cast shame aside and made that declaration at the party—more particularly, it was to save the situation for her friend, who had been fidgeting about and looking conspicuously guilty. But what was she to think now? Beneath the peculiarity of Mrs. Kasuga's whole attitude, and beneath this elaborate procedure of having herself accompany her as she returned the pearl, she sensed that there lay something much deeper. Could it be that Mrs. Azuma's intuition had touched upon a weakness in her friend's make-up which it was forbidden to touch upon and that by thus driving her friend into a corner, she had transformed an unconscious, impulsive kleptomania into a deep mental derangement beyond all cure?

Mrs. Kasuga, for her part, still retained the suspicion that

Mrs. Azuma had genuinely swallowed the pearl and that her confession at the party had been the truth. If that was so, it had been unforgivable of Mrs. Azuma, when everything was smoothly settled, to tease her so cruelly on the way back from the party, shifting the guilt onto herself. As a result, timid creature that she was, she had been panic-stricken and, besides spending good money, had felt obliged to act out that little play—and was it not exceedingly ill-natured of Mrs. Azuma that even after all this, she still refused to confess it was she who had eaten the pearl? And if Mrs. Azuma's innocence was all pretense, she herself—acting her part so painstakingly—must appear in Mrs. Azuma's eyes as the most ridiculous of third-rate comedians.

To return to Mrs. Matsumura: That lady, on her way back from obliging Mrs. Sasaki to accept the pearl, was feeling now more at ease in her mind and had the notion to make a leisurely reinvestigation, detail by detail, of the events of the recent incident. When going to collect her portion of the cake, she had most certainly left her handbag on the chair. Then, while eating the cake, she had more liberal use of the paper napkin—so there could have been no necessity to take a handkerchief from her bag. The more she thought about it, the less she could remember having opened her bag until she touched up her face in the taxi on the way home. How was it, then, that a pearl had rolled into a handbag which was always shut?

She realized now how stupid she had been not to have remarked this simple fact before, instead of flying into a panic at the mere sight of the pearl. Having progressed this far, Mrs. Matsumura was struck by an amazing thought. Someone must purposely have placed the pearl in her bag in order to incriminate her. And of the four guests at the party, the only one who would do such a thing was, without doubt, the detestable Mrs. Yamamoto. Her eyes glinting with rage, Mrs. Matsumura hurried toward the house of Mrs. Yamamoto.

From her first glimpse of Mrs. Matsumura standing in the doorway, Mrs. Yamamoto knew at once what had brought her. She had already prepared her line of defense.

However, Mrs. Matsumura's cross-examination was unexpectedly severe, and from the start it was clear that she would accept no evasions.

"It was you, I know. No one but you could do such a thing," began Mrs. Matsumura, deductively.

"Why choose me? What proof have you? If you can say a thing

like that to my face, I suppose you've come with pretty conclusive proof, have you?" Mrs. Yamamoto was at first icily composed.

To this Mrs. Matsumura replied that Mrs. Azuma, having so nobly taken the blame on herself, clearly stood in an incompatible relationship with mean and despicable behavior of this nature; and as for Mrs. Kasuga, she was much too weak-kneed for such dangerous work; and that left only one person—herself.

Mrs. Yamamoto kept silent, her mouth shut tight like a clamshell. On the table before her gleamed the pearl which Mrs. Matsumura had set there. In the excitement she had not even had time to raise a teaspoon, and the Ceylon tea she had so thoughtfully provided was beginning to get cold.

"I had no idea that you hated me so." As she said this, Mrs. Yamamoto dabbed at the corners of her eyes, but it was plain that Mrs. Matsumura's resolve not to be deceived by tears was as firm as ever.

"Well, then," Mrs. Yamamoto continued, "I shall say what I had thought I must never say. I shall mention no names, but one of the guests . . ."

"By that, I suppose, you can only mean Mrs. Azuma or Mrs. Kasuga?"

"Please, I beg at least that you allow me to omit the name. As I say, one of the guests had just opened your bag and was dropping something inside when I happened to glance in her direction. You can imagine my amazement! Even if I had felt *able* to warn you, there would have been no chance. My heart just throbbed and throbbed, and on the way back in the taxi—oh, how awful not to be able to speak even then! If we had been good friends, of course, I could have told you quite frankly, but since I knew of your apparent dislike for me . . .:"

"I see. You have been very considerate, I'm sure. Which means, doesn't it, that you have now cleverly shifted the blame onto Mrs. Azuma and Mrs. Kasuga?"

"Shifted the blame! Oh, how can I get you to understand my feelings? I only wanted to avoid hurting anyone."

"Quite. But you didn't mind hurting me, did you? You might at least have mentioned this in the taxi."

"And if you had been frank with me when you found the pearl in your bag, I would probably have told you, at that moment, everything I had seen—but no, you chose to leave the taxi at once, without saying a word!"

For the first time, as she listened to this, Mrs. Matsumura was at a loss for a reply.

"Well, then. Can I get you to understand? I wanted no one to be hurt."

Mrs. Matsumura was filled with an even more intense rage.

"If you are going to tell a string of lies like that," she said, "I must ask you to repeat them, tonight if you wish, in my presence, before Mrs. Azuma and Mrs. Kasuga."

At this Mrs. Yamamoto started to weep.

"And thanks to you," she sobbed reprovingly, "all my efforts to avoid hurting anyone will have come to nothing."

It was a new experience for Mrs. Matsumura to see Mrs. Yamamoto crying, and though she kept reminding herself not to be taken in by tears, she could not altogether dismiss the feeling that perhaps somewhere, since nothing in this affair could be proved, there might be a modicum of truth even in the assertions of Mrs. Yamamoto.

In the fist place—to be a little more objective—if one accepted Mrs. Yamamoto's story as true, then her reluctance to disclose the name of the guilty party, whom she had observed in the very act, argued some refinement of character. And just as one could not say for sure that the gentle and seemingly timid Mrs. Kasuga would never be moved to an act of malice, so even the undoubtedly bad feeling between Mrs. Yamamoto and herself could, by one way of looking at things, be taken as actually lessening the likelihood of Mrs. Yamamoto's guilt. For if she was to do a thing like this, with their relationship as it was, Mrs. Yamamoto would be the first to come under suspicion.

"We have differences in our natures," Mrs. Yamamoto continued tearfully, "and I cannot deny that there are things about yourself which I dislike. But for all that, it is really too bad that you should suspect me of such a petty trick to get the better of you. . . . Still, on thinking it over, to submit quietly to your accusations might well be the course most consistent with what I have felt in this matter all along. In this way I alone shall bear the guilt, and no other will be hurt."

After this pathetic pronouncement, Mrs. Yamamoto lowered her face to the table and abandoned herself to uncontrolled weeping.

Watching her, Mrs. Matsumura came, by degrees, to reflect upon the impulsiveness of her own behavior. Detesting Mrs. Yamamoto as she had, there had been times in her castigation of that lady when she had allowed herself to be blinded by emotion.

When Mrs. Yamamoto raised her head again after this prolonged bout of weeping, the look of resolution on her face, somehow remote and pure, was apparent even to her visitor. Mrs.

Matsumura, a little frightened, drew herself upright in her chair.

"This thing should never have been. When it is gone, everything will be as before." Speaking in riddles, Mrs. Yamamoto pushed back her disheveled hair and fixed a terrible, yet hauntingly beautiful, gaze upon the top of the table. In an instant she had snatched up the pearl from before her and, with a gesture of no ordinary resolve, tossed it into her mouth. Raising her cup by the handle, her little finger elegantly extended, she washed the pearl down her throat with one gulp of cold Ceylon tea.

Mrs. Matsumura watched in horrified fascination. The affair was over before she had time to protest. This was the first time in her life she had seen a person swallow a pearl, and there was in Mrs. Yamamoto's manner something of that desperate finality one might expect to see in a person who had just drunk poison.

However, heroic though the action was, it was above all a touching incident, and not only did Mrs. Matsumura find her anger vanished into thin air, but so impressed was she by Mrs. Yamamoto's simplicity and purity that she could only think of that lady as a saint. And now Mrs. Matsumura's eyes too began to fill with tears, and she took Mrs. Yamamoto by the hand.

"Please forgive me, please forgive me," she said. "It was wrong of me."

For a while they wept together, holding each other's hands and vowing to each other that henceforth they would be the firmest of friends.

When Mrs. Sasaki heard rumors that the relationship between Mrs. Yamamoto and Mrs. Matsumura, which had been so strained, had suddenly improved, and that Mrs. Azuma and Mrs. Kasuga, who had been such good friends, had suddenly fallen out, she was at a loss to understand the reasons and contented herself with the reflection that nothing was impossible in this world.

However, being a woman of no strong scruples, Mrs. Sasaki requested a jeweler to refashion her ring and to produce a design into which two new pearls could be set, one large and one small, and this she wore quite openly, without further mishap.

Soon she had completely forgotten the small commotion on her birthday, and when anyone asked her age, she would give the same untruthful answers as ever.

from
From Emperor to Citizen

Aisin-Gioro P'u Yi

THE "Articles for Favorable Treatment" stipulated that I could live temporarily in the Imperial Palace without fixing any definite time limit. Apart from three large halls that were handed over to the Republic, the rest of the Forbidden City continued to belong to the Imperial Palace. It was in this tiny world that I was to spend the most absurd childhood possible until I was driven out by the soldiers of the National Army in 1924. I call it absurd because at a time when China was called a republic and mankind had advanced into the twentieth century, I was still living the life of an emperor, breathing the dust of the nineteenth century.

Whenever I think of my childhood, my head fills with a yellow mist. The glazed tiles were yellow, my sedan chair was yellow, my chair cushions were yellow, the linings of my hats and clothes were yellow, the girdle round my waist was yellow, the dishes and bowls from which I ate and drank, the padded cover of the rice-gruel saucepan, the material in which my books were wrapped, the window curtains, the bridle of my horse . . . everything was yellow. This color, the so-called "brilliant yellow," was used exclusively by the imperial household and made me feel from my earliest years that I was unique and had a "heavenly" nature different from that of everybody else.

When I was ten; my grandmother and mother started to come and visit me on the orders of the High Consorts, and they brought my brother Pu Chieh and my first sister to play with me for a few days. Their first visit started off very drearily: I and my grandmother sat on the *kang,* and she watched me playing dominoes while my brother and sister stood below us very properly, gazing at me with a fixed stare like attendants on duty in a *yamen.* Later it occurred to me to take them along to the part of the palace in which I lived, where I asked Pu Chieh, "What games do you play at home?"

"Pu Chieh can play hide-and-seek," said my brother, who was a year younger than I, in a very respectful way.

"So you play hide-and-seek too? It's a jolly good game." I was

very excited. I had played it with the eunuchs but never with children younger than myself. So we started to play hide-and-seek, and in the excitement of the game, my brother and sister forgot their inhibitions. We deliberately let down the blinds to make the room very dark. My sister, who was two years younger than I, was at the same time enraptured and terrified, and as my brother and I kept giving her frights, we got so carried away that we were laughing and shouting. When we were exhausted, we climbed up onto the *kang* to get our breath back, and I told them to think of some new game. Pu Chieh was thoughtful for a while, then started to gaze at me wordlessly, a silly smile on his face.

"What are you grinning at?"

He went on grinning.

"Tell me! Tell me!" I urged him impatiently, thinking that he must certainly have thought out some new game. To my surprise he came out with, "I thought, oh, Pu Chieh thought that Your Majesty would be different from ordinary people. The emperors on the stage have long beards. . . ." As he spoke, he pretended to be stroking his beard.

This gesture was his undoing. As he raised his hand, I noticed that the lining of his sleeve was a very familiar color. My face blackened.

"Pu Chieh, are you allowed to wear that color?"

"But . . . bu . . . but isn't it apricot?"

"Nonsense! It's imperial brilliant yellow."

"Yes, sire, yes, sire. . . ." Pu Chieh stood away from me, his arms hanging respectfully by his sides. My sister slipped over to stand with him, frightened to the point of tears.

"It's brilliant yellow. You have no business to be wearing it."

"Yes, sire."

With his "yes, sire" my brother reverted to being my subject. The sound "yes, sire" died out long ago, and it seems very funny when one thinks of it today. But I got used to it from early childhood, and if people did not use the words when replying to me, I would not stand for it. It was the same with kneeling and kowtowing. From my infancy I was accustomed to having people kowtow to me, particularly people over ten times my own age. They included old officials of the Ching Dynasty and the elders of my own clan, men in the court robes of the Ching Dynasty and officials of the Republic in Western dress.

Another strange thing which seemed quite normal at the time was the daily pomp.

Every time I went to my schoolroom to study, or visited the High Consorts to pay my respects, or went for a stroll in the garden, I was always followed by a large retinue. Every trip I made to the Summer Palace must have cost thousands of Mexican dollars: the Republic's police had to be asked to line the roads to protect me, and I was accompanied by a motorcade consisting of dozens of vehicles.

Whenever I went for a stroll in the garden, a procession had to be organized. In front went a eunuch from the Administrative Bureau whose function was roughly that of a motor horn: he walked twenty or thirty yards ahead of the rest of the party intoning the sound "chir . . . chir . . ." as a warning to anyone who might be in the vicinity to go away at once. Next came two chief eunuchs, advancing crabwise on either side of the path; ten paces behind them came the center of the procession—the Empress Dowager or myself. If I was being carried in a chair, there would be two junior eunuchs walking beside me to attend to my wants at any moment; if I was walking, they would be supporting me. Next came a eunuch with a large silk canopy followed by a large group of eunuchs of whom some were empty-handed and others were holding all sorts of things: a seat in case I wanted to rest, changes of clothing, umbrellas and parasols. After these eunuchs of the imperial presence came eunuchs of the imperial tea bureau with boxes of various kinds of cakes and delicacies and, of course, jugs of hot water and a tea service; they were followed by eunuchs of the imperial dispensary bearing cases of medicine and first-aid equipment suspended from carrying poles. The medicines carried always included potions prepared from lampwick sedge, chrysanthemums, the roots of reeds, bamboo leaves, and bamboo skins; in summer there were always Essence of Betony Pills for Rectifying the Vapor, Six Harmony Pills for Stabilizing the Center, Gold coated, Heat-dispersing Cinnabar, Fragrant Herb Pills, Omnipurpose Bars, colic medicine and antiplague powder; and throughout all four seasons there would be the Three Immortals Beverage to aid the digestion, as well as many other medicaments. At the end of the procession came the eunuchs who carried commodes and chamber pots. If I was walking, a sedan chair, open or covered according to the season, would bring up the rear. This motley procession of several dozen people would proceed in perfect silence and order.

But I would often throw it into confusion. When I was young, I liked to run around when I was in high spirits as just any child

does. At first they would all scuttle along after me puffing and panting with their procession reduced to chaos. When I grew a little older and knew how to give orders, I would tell them to stand and wait for me; then, apart from the junior eunuchs of the imperial presence who came with me, they would all stand there waiting in silence with their loads. After I had finished running around, they would form up again behind me. When I learn to ride a bicycle and ordered the removal of all the upright wooden thresholds in the palace so that I could ride around without obstruction, the procession was no longer able to follow me, and so it had to be temporarily abolished. But when I went to pay my respects to the High Consorts or to my schoolroom, I still had to have something of a retinue, and without it I would have felt rather odd. When I heard people telling the story of the last emperor of the Ming Dynasty who had only one eunuch left with him at the end, I felt very uncomfortable.

The type of extravagant display that wasted the most effort, money and material was meals. There were special terms to refer to the emperor's eating, and it was absolutely forbidden to fail to use them correctly. Food was called not "food" but "viands"; eating was called "consuming viands"; serving the meal was "transmitting the viands"; and the kitchen was the "imperial viands room." When it was time to eat (and the times of the meals were not set but were whenever the emperor felt like eating), I would give the command "Transmit the viands!" The junior eunuchs of the presence would then repeat "Transmit the viands" to the eunuchs standing in the main hall of the palace in which I lived, and they would pass it on to the eunuchs standing on duty outside the hall; these would in turn call it out to the eunuchs of the "imperial viands room" waiting in the Western Avenue of the Forbidden City. Thus my order went straight to the kitchens, and before its echoes had died away a procession rather of the sort that used to take a bride's trousseau to her groom's house had already issued from the "viands room." It was made up of an imposing column of several dozen neatly dressed eunuchs hurrying to the Mind Nurture Palace with seven tables of various sizes and scores of red-lacquered boxes painted with golden dragons. When they reached the main hall, they handed their burdens over to young eunuchs wearing white sleeves, who laid out the meal in an eastern room of the palace.

Usually there were two tables of main dishes with another one

of chafing dishes added in winter; there were three tables with cakes, rice and porridge, respectively; and there was another small table of salted vegetables. All the crockery was imperial yellow porcelain with dragon designs and the words "Ten thousand long lives without limit" painted on it. In winter I ate from silver dishes placed on top of porcelain bowls of hot water. Every dish or bowl had a strip of silver on it as a precaution against poison, and for the same reason all the food was tasted by a eunuch before it was brought in. This was called "appraising the viands." When everything had been tasted and laid out, and before I took my place, a young eunuch would call out "Remove the covers." This was the signal for four or five other junior eunuchs to take the silver lids off all the food dishes, put them in a large box and carry them out. I then began to "use the viands."

And what was the food laid out "ten cubits square"? The empress dowager Lung Yu would have about a hundred main dishes on six tables, an extravagance inherited from the empress dowager Tzu Hsi. I had about thirty. But these dishes which were brought in with such ceremonial were only for show. The reason why the food could be served almost as soon as I gave the word was that it had been prepared several hours or even a whole day in advance and was being kept warm over the kitchen stoves. The cooks knew that at least since the time of Kuang Hsu, the emperor had not eaten this food. The food I ate was sent over by the Empress Dowager, and after her death, by the High Consorts. She and each of the High Consorts had kitchens of their own staffed by highly skilled chefs who produced twenty or more really delicious dishes for every meal. This was the food that was put in front of me, while that prepared by the imperial kitchens was set some distance away as it was only there for the sake of appearances.

To show how they loved and cared for me, the High Consorts also sent a responsible eunuch to report on how I had "consumed viands." This too was a pure formality. No matter what I had really eaten, the eunuch would go to the quarters of the High Consorts, kneel before them and say:

"Your slave reports to his masters: the Lord of Ten Thousand Years consumed one bowl of old rice viands (or white rice viands), one steamed breadroll (or a griddle cake) and a bowl of congee. He consumed it with relish."

At Chinese New Year and other festivals and on the birthdays of the High Consorts, my kitchen sent a spread of food to the

Consorts as a mark of my filial piety. This food could be described as expensive and showy without being good, and was neither nutritious nor tasty.

According to the record of one month of the second year of my reign, the empress dowager Lung Yu, the four High Consorts and myself used up 3,960 catties of meat (over two tons) and 388 chickens and ducks every month, of which 810 catties and 240 chickens and ducks were for me, a four-year-old child. In addition there was a monthly allocation for the numerous people in the palace who served us: members of the Grand Council, imperial bodyguards, tutors, Hanlin academicians, painters, men who drew the outlines of characters for others to fill in, important eunuchs, *shaman* magicians who came every day to sacrifice to the spirits, and many others. Including the Dowager, the Consorts and myself, the monthly consumption of pork was 14,642 catties at a cost of 2,342.72 taels of silver. On top of this there were the extra dishes we had every day, which often cost several times as much again. In the month in question there were 31,844 catties of extra meat, 814 catties of extra pork fat and 4,786 extra chickens and ducks, to say nothing of the fish, shrimps and eggs. All these extras cost 11,641.07 taels, and with miscellaneous items added, the total expenditure came to 14,794.19 taels. It is obvious that all this money (except what was embezzled) was wasted in order to display the grandeur of the emperor. This figure, moreover, does not include the cost of the cakes, fruit, sweets and drinks that were constantly being devoured.

Just as food was cooked in huge quantities but not eaten, so was a vast amount of clothing made which was never worn. I cannot now remember much about this, but I do know that while the Dowager and the High Consorts had fixed yearly allocations, there were no limits for the emperor, for whom clothes were constantly made throughout the year. I do not know what exactly was made, but everything I wore was always new. I have before me an account from an unspecified year headed "List of materials actually used in making clothes for His Majesty's use from the sixth day of the eleventh month." According to this list the following garments were made for me that month: eleven fur jackets, six fur inner and outer gowns, two fur waistcoats, and thirty padded waistcoats and pairs of trousers. Leaving aside the cost of the main materials and of the labor, the bill for such minor items as the edgings, pockets, buttons and thread came

to 2,137.6335 silver dollars.

My changes of clothing were all laid down in regulations and were the responsibility of the eunuchs of the clothing store-rooms. Even my everyday gowns came in twenty-eight different styles, from the one in black and white inlaid fur that I started wearing on the nineteenth of the first lunar month to the sable one I changed into on the first day of the eleventh month. Needless to say, my clothes were far more complicated on festivals and ceremonial occasions.

To manage all this extravagant pomp there was, of course, a suitable proliferation of offices and personnel. The Household Department, which administered the domestic affairs of the emperor, had under its control seven bureaus and forty-eight offices. The seven bureaus—the storage bureau, the guard bureau, the protocol, the counting house, the stock-raising bureau, the disciplinary bureau and the construction bureau—all had storerooms, workshops and so on under them. The storage bureau, for example, was for stores for silver, fur, porcelain, satin, clothes and tea. According to a list of officials dating from 1909, the personnel of the Household Department numbered 1,023 (excluding the Palace Guard, the eunuchs and the servants known as "sulas"); in the early years of the Republic, this number was reduced to something over 600, and at the time I left the Imperial Palace there were still more than 300. It is not hard to imagine an organization as large as this with so many people in it, but the triviality of some of its functions was almost unthinkable. One of the forty-eight offices, for example, was the As You Wish Lodge (Ju Yi Kuan). Its only purpose was to paint pictures and do calligraphy for the Empress Dowager and the High Consorts; if the Dowager wanted to paint something, the As You Wish Lodge would outline a design for her so that all she had to do was to fill in the colors and write a title on it. The calligraphy for large tablets was sketched out by the experts of the Great Diligence Hall or else done by the Hanlin academicians. Nearly all late Ching inscriptions that purport to be the brush-work of a dowager or an emperor were produced in this way.

The buildings all around me and the furniture of the palace were all a part of my indoctrination. Apart from the golden-glazed tiles that were exclusively for the use of the emperor, the very height of the buildings was an imperial prerogative that served to teach me from an early age that not only was everything under heaven the emperor's land but even the sky above my head be-

longed to nobody else. Every piece of furniture was "direct method" teaching material for me. It was said that the emperor Chien Lung once laid it down that nothing in the palace, not even a blade of grass, must be lost. To put this principle into practice, he put some blades of grass on a table in the palace and gave orders that they were to be counted every day to see that not a single one of them was missing. This was called "taking the grass as a standard." Even in my time these thirty-six withered blades of grass were still preserved in a cloisonné canister in the Mind Nurture Palace. This grass filled me with unbounded admiration for my ancestor and unbridled hatred for the Revolution of 1911.

There is no longer any way of calculating exactly the enormous cost of the daily life of an emperor, but a record called "A comparison between the expenditure of the seventh year of Hsuan Tung (1915) and the past three years" compiled by the Household Department shows that expenditure in 1915 topped 2,790,000 taels and that, while it dropped in each of the following three years, it was always over 1,890,000 taels. Thus it was that with the connivance of the Republican authorities we continued our prodigious waste of the sweat and blood of the people in order to maintain our former pomp and continue our parasitic way of life.

Some of the rules in the palace were originally not simply for the sake of show. The system by which all the food dishes had strips of silver on them and the food was tasted before the emperor ate it and the large-scale security precautions [were taken] whenever he went out was basically to protect him against any attempt on his life. It was said that the reason why emperors had no outside privies was that one emperor had been set upon by an assassin when going out to relieve himself. These stories and all the display had the same effect on me: they made me believe that I was a very important and august person, a man apart who ruled and owned the universe.

In the Land of Small Dragon: A Vietnamese Folk Tale

Told by Dang Manh Kha

One

Man cannot know the whole world,
But can know his own small part.
In the Land of Small Dragon,
In the Year of the Chicken,
In a Village of No-Name,
In the bend of the river,
There were many small houses
Tied together by walkways.
Mulberry and apricot,
Pear tree and flowering vine
Dropped their delicate blossoms
On a carpet of new grass.
In a Village of No-Name
Lived a man and two daughters.
T'âm was the elder daughter;
Her mother died at her birth.
A jewel box of gold and jade
Holds only jewels of great price.
T'âm's face was a golden moon,
Her eyes dark as a storm cloud,
Her feet delicate flowers
Stepping lightly on the wind.
No envy lived in her heart,
Nor bitterness in her tears.
Cám was the younger daughter,
Child of Number Two Wife.
Cám's face was long and ugly,
Scowling and discontented,
Frowning in deep displeasure.
Indolent, slow and idle,
Her heart was filled with hatred
For her beautiful sister.
An evil heart keeps records

On the face of its owner.
The father loved both daughters,
One not more than the other.
He did not permit his heart
To call one name more dearly.
He lived his days in justice,
Standing strong against the wind.
Father had a little land,
A house made of mats and clay,
A grove of mulberry trees
Enclosed by growing bamboo,
A garden and rice paddy,
Two great water buffalo,
A well for drinking water,
And twin fish ponds for the fish.
Cám's mother, Number Two Wife,
Cared only for her own child.
Her mind had only one thought:
What would give pleasure to Cám.
Her heart had only one door
And only Cám could enter.
Number Two Wife was jealous
Of T'âm, the elder daughter,
Who ws beautiful and good,
So the mother planned revenge
On the good, beautiful child.
To Cám she gave everything,
But nothing but work to T'âm.
T'âm carried water buckets,
Hanging from her bamboo pole.
T'âm carried forest fagots
To burn in the kitchen fire.
T'âm transplanted young rice plants
From seed bed to rice paddy.
T'âm flailed the rice on a rock,
Then she winnowed and gleaned it.
T'âm's body ached with tiredness,
Her heart was heavy and sad.
She said, "Wise Father, listen!
I am your elder daughter;
Therefore why may I not be
Number One Daughter, also?

"A Number One Daughter works,
But she works with dignity.
If I were your Number One
The honor would ease my pain.
As it is, I am a slave,
Without honor or dignity."
Waiting for wisdom to come,
Father was slow to give answer.
"Both my daughters share my heart.
I cannot choose between them.
One of you must earn the right
To be my Number One child."
A man's worth is what he does,
Not what he says he can do.
"Go, Daughters, to the fish pond;
Take your fish baskets with you.
Fish until night moon-mist comes.
Bring your fish catch back to me.
She who brings a full basket
Is my Number One Daughter.
Your work, not my heart, decides
Your place in your father's house."
T'âm listened to her father
And was quick to obey him.
With her basket, she waded
In the mud of the fish pond.
With quick-moving, graceful hands
She caught the quick-darting fish.
Slowly the long hours went by.
Slowly her fish basket filled.
Cám sat on the high, dry bank
Trying to think of some plan,
Her basket empty of fish,
But her mind full of cunning.
"I, wade in that mud?" she thought.
"There must be some better way."
At last she knew what to do
To be Number One Daughter.
"T'âm," she called, "elder sister,
Our father needs a bright flower,
A flower to gladden his heart.
Get it for him, dear sister."

T'âm, the good, gentle sister,
Set her fish basket aside
And ran into the forest
To pick the night-blooming flowers.
Cám crept to T'âm's fish basket,
Emptied it into her own.
Now her fish basket was full.
T'âm's held only one small fish.
Quickly Cám ran to Father,
Calling, "See my full basket!"
T'âm ran back to the fish pond
With an armload of bright flowers.
"Cám," she called, "what has happened?
What has happened to my fish?"
Slowly T'âm went to Father
Bringing him the flowers and fish.
Father looked at both baskets.
Speaking slowly, he told them,
"The test was a full basket,
Not flowers and one small fish.
Take your fish, Elder Daughter.
It is much too small to eat.
Cám has earned the right to be
Honorable Number One."

Two
T'âm looked at the little fish.
Her heart was filled with pity
At its loneliness and fright.
"Little fish, dear little fish,
I will put you in the well."
At night T'âm brought her rice bowl,
Sharing her food with the fish—
Talked to the thin fish, saying,
"Little fish, come eat with me"—
Stayed at the well at nighttime
With the stars for company.
The fish grew big and trustful.
It grew fat and not afraid.
It knew T'âm's voice and answered,
Swimming to her outstretched hand.
Cám sat in the dark shadows,

Her heart full of jealousy,
Her mind full of wicked thoughts.
Sweetly she called, "T'âm, sister.
Our father is overtired.
Come sing him a pretty song
That will bring sweet dreams to him."
Quickly T'âm ran to her father,
Singing him a nightbird song.
Cám was hiding near the well,
Watching, waiting and watching.
When she heard T'âm's pretty song
She crept closer to the fish,
Whispering, "Dear little fish,
Come to me! Come eat with me."
The fish came, and greedy Cám
Touched it, caught it and ate it!
T'âm returned. Her fish was gone.
"Little fish, dear little fish,
Come to me! Come eat with me!"
Bitterly she cried for it.
The stars looked down in pity;
The clouds shed teardrops of rain.

Three
T'âm's tears falling in the well
Made the water rise higher.
And from it rose Nâng Tien,
A lovely cloud-dressed fairy.
Her voice was a silver bell
Ringing clear in the moonlight.
"My child, why are you crying?"
"My dear little fish is gone!
He does not come when I call."
"Ask Red Rooster to help you.
His hens will find Little Fish."
Soon the hens came in a line
Sadly bringing the fish bones.
T'âm cried, holding the fish bones.
"Your dear fish will not forget.
Place his bones in a clay pot
Safe beneath your sleeping mat.
Those we love never leave us.

Cherished bones keep love alive."
In her treasured clay pot, T'âm
Made a bed of flower petals
For the bones of Little Fish
And put him away with love.
But she did not forget him;
When the moon was full again,
T'âm, so lonely for her fish,
Dug up the buried clay pot.
T'âm found, instead of fish bones,
A silken dress and two jeweled *hai.*
Her Nâng Tien spoke again.
"Your dear little fish loves you.
Clothe yourself in the garments
His love has given you."
T'âm put on the small jeweled *hai.*
They fit like a velvet skin
Made of moonlight and stardust
And the love of Little Fish.
T'âm heard music in her heart
That sent her small feet dancing,
Flitting like two butterflies,
Skimming like two flying birds,
Dancing by the twin fish ponds,
Dancing in the rice paddy.
But the mud in the rice paddy
Kept one jeweled *hai* for its own.
Night Wind brought the *hai* to T'âm.
"What is yours I bring to you."
Water in the well bubbled,
"I will wash your *hai* for you."
Water buffalo came by.
"Dry your *hai* on my sharp horn."
A blackbird flew by singing,
"I know where this *hai* belongs.
In a garden far away
I will take this *hai* for you."

Four
What is to be must happen
As day follows after night.
In the Emperor's garden,

Sweet with perfume of roses,
The Emperor's son, the Prince,
Walked alone in the moonlight.
A bird, black against the moon,
Flew along the garden path,
Dropping a star in its flight.
"Look! A star!" exclaimed the Prince.
Carefully he picked it up
And found it was the small jeweled *hai.*
"Only a beautiful maid
Can wear this beautiful *hai.*"
The Prince whispered to his heart,
And his heart answered, "Find her."
In truth, beauty seeks goodness:
What is beautiful is good.
The Prince went to his father:
"A bird dropped this at my feet.
Surely it must come as truth,
Good and fair the maid it fits.
Sire, if it is your pleasure
I would take this maid for wife."
The Great Emperor was pleased
With the wishes of his son.
He called his servants to him,
His drummers and his crier,
Proclaiming a Festival
To find one who owned the *hai.*
In the Village of No-Name
The Emperor's subjects heard—
They heard the Royal Command.
There was praise and rejoicing.
They were pleased the Royal Son
Would wed one of their daughters.

Five
Father's house was filled with clothes,
Embroidered *áo-dài* and *hai*
Of heavy silks and rich colors.
Father went outside to sit.
Cám and her mother whispered
Their hopes, their dreams and their plans.
Cám, Number One Daughter, asked,

"Mother, will the Prince choose me?"
Mother said, "Of course he will.
You will be the fairest there!
When you curtsy to the Prince
His heart will go out to you."
T'âm, Daughter Number Two, said,
"May I go with you and Cám?"
Cám's mother answered curtly,
"Yes, if you have done this task:
Separating rice and husks
From one basket into two."
T'âm knew Cám's mother had mixed
The cleaned rice with rice unhusked.
She looked at the big basket
Full to brim with rice and husks.
Separating the cleaned rice
From that of rice unhusked
Would take all harvest moon time,
When the Festival would end.
A cloud passed over the moon.
Whirring wings outsung the wind.
A flock of blackbirds lighted
On the pile of leaves and grain.
Picking the grain from the leaves,
They dropped clean rice at T'âm's feet.
T'âm could almost not believe
That the endless task was done.
T'âm, the elder daughter, said,
"May I go? May I go, too,
Now that all my work is done?"
Cám taunted, "How could you go?
You have nothing fit to wear."
"If I had a dress to wear
Could I go to the Palace?"
"If wishes were dresses, yes,
But wishes are not dresses."
When Mother left she said,
"Our dear Cám is ravishing.
Stay at home, you Number Two!
Cám will be the one to wed."
T'âm dug up the big clay pot
The dress and one *hai* were there—

As soft as misty moon clouds,
Delicate as rose perfume.
T'âm washed her face in the well,
Combed her hair by the fish pond.
She smoothed down the silken dress,
Tied one *hai* unto her belt
And, though her feet were bare,
Hurried, scurried, ran and ran.
She ran to the Festival
In the King's Royal Garden.
At the Palace gates the Guards
Bowed before her, very low.
Pretty girls stood in a line
With their mothers standing near;
One by one they tried to fit
A foot into a small, jeweled *hai.*
Cám stood beside her mother,
By the gilded throne-room door.
Her face was dark and angry
Like a brooding monsoon wind.
Cám, wiping her tears away,
Sobbed and whimpered and complained,
"My small foot fits his old shoe—
Everything but my big toe."
T'âm stood shyly by the door
Looking in great wonderment
While trumpeters and drummers
Made music for her entrance.
People looked at gentle T'âm.
Everyone was whispering,
"Oh! She is so beautiful!
She must be a Princess fair
From some distant foreign land."
Then the Prince looked up and saw
A lady walking toward him.
Stepping from his Royal Throne,
He quickly went to meet her,
And taking her hand led her
To His Majesty the King.
What is to be must happen
As day happens after night.
Real beauty mirrors goodness.

What is one is the other.
Kneeling, the Prince placed the *hai*
On T'âm's dainty little foot.
T'âm untied the *hai* she wore
And slid her bare foot in it.
Beauty is not painted on.
It is the spirit showing.
The Prince spoke to his father.
"I would take this maid for wife."
His Royal Highness nodded.
"We will have a Wedding Feast."
All the birds in all the trees
Sang a song of happiness:
"T'âm, the Number Two Daughter,
Is to be Wife Number One."
That is written in the stars
Cannot be changed or altered.

The Nose

Akutagawa Ryunosuke

Translated by Takashi Kojima

IN the town of Ike-no-O there was no one who had not heard of Zenchi Naigu's nose. Dangling from his upper lip to below his chin, five or six inches long, it was of the same thickness from end to end.

For fifty years he had been tormented at heart by the presence of his nose—from his young days as an acolyte until the time he rose to the respected office of Palace Chaplain. To others he tried to appear unconcerned about his nose, not so much because his preoccupation with such a matter was not worthy of a man whose duty it was to devote himself ardently to prayer for the advent of Paradise as because he wished to keep from the knowledge of others that he was worried over his nose. With him his apparent concern was rather a matter of pride, and his greatest dread in everyday conversation was to hear the word *nose.*

His nose was, of course, an intolerable nuisance. In the first place, he could not take his meals by himself. If he tried, the tip of his nose would reach down into the boiled rice in his bowl. So at meals he had to have one of his disciples sit opposite him and hold up the end of his nose with an oblong piece of wood about two feet long and an inch wide. This manner of taking meals was, of course, no easy matter for the priest whose nose was held up or for his disciple who held it up.

Once a page, who was acting in the place of the disciple, happened to sneeze and dropped the nose into the bowl—this incident was talked about as far as Kyoto. He could accept the practical inconvenience of having a long nose, but the loss of his dignity on account of it was intolerable.

The Ike-no-O townspeople used to say that it was fortunate for the priest that he was not a layman, for surely no woman would care to be the wife of a man who had such a nose. Some went so far as to say that were it not for his nose, he might not have taken holy orders.

He did not consider that his priesthood had been a refuge which offered him any service in lightening the burden of his nose. Moreover his pride was too delicately strung for him to be

influenced in the least by such a worldly eventuality as matrimony. His sole concern was to resort to every possible means to heal the wounds his pride had suffered and to repair the losses his dignity had sustained.

He exhausted all possible means to make his nose appear shorter than it really was. When there was no one about, he would examine his nose in the mirror and look at it from various angles, taxing his ingenuity to the utmost. Just changing the reflections of his face in the mirror was not enough: prodding his cheeks, or putting his finger on the tip of his chin, he would patiently study his face in the mirror. But not once could he satisfy himself that his nose was shorter. Indeed, it often happened that the more he studied his nose the longer it seemed to be. On such occasions, he would put his mirror back into its box, sighing heavily, and sadly going back to his lectern would continue chanting the sutra to Kwannon, or the Goddess of Mercy.

He paid close attention to other people's noses. The Temple of Ike-no-O, frequented by a large number of visitors, both priests and laymen, held Buddhist masses, receptions for visiting priests, and sermons for parishioners. The precincts of the Temple were lined with closely built cells, with a bathhouse which had heated water daily. He would closely scrutinize the visitors, patiently trying to find at least one person who might possibly have a nose like his own in order that he might ease his troubled mind. He took no notice of the rich silken attire, the ordinary hempen clothes, the priests' saffron hoods nor their dark sacerdotal robes, all of which counted for next to nothing in his eyes. That which arrested his eyes was not the people or their attire but their noses. He could find hooked noses but none like his own. Each additional failure made his thinking darker and gloomier.

While talking with others, unconsciously he would take between his fingers the tip of his dangling nose; then he would blush with shame for an act ill fitting his years and office. His misfortune had driven him to such extremes.

In his desperate attempt to find some consolation by discovering someone with a nose like his own, he delved into the voluminous Buddhist scriptures; but in all the scriptures there was not one reference to a long nose. How comforting it would have been to find, for instance, that either Mu Lien or Sha Lien had a long nose.

He did find that King Liu Hsan-ti of the Kingdom of Chu-han in the third century A.D. had long ears, and thought how reassuring it would have been if it had happened that the King's nose, instead of his ears, had been long.

It need hardly be said that while taking assiduous pains to seek spiritual consolation, he did try most earnestly a variety of elaborate practical measures to shorten his nose. At one time he took a concoction with a snake-gourd base. At another he bathed his nose in the urine of mice; yet with all his persistent and unremitting efforts, he still had five to six inches of nose dangling down over his lips.

One autumn day a disciple went on a trip to Kyoto, partly on his master's business, and before his returning to Ike-no-O, his physician acquaintance happened to introduce him to the mysteries of shortening noses. The physician, who had come to Japan from China, was at that time a priest attached to the Choraku Temple.

Zenchi, with an assumed nonchalance, avoided calling for an immediate test of the remedy, and could only drop casual hints about his regret that he must cause his disciple so much bother at meals, although he eagerly waited in his heart for his disciple to persuade him to try the remedy. The disciple could not fail to see through his master's design. But his master's innermost feelings, which led him to work out such an elaborate scheme, aroused his disciple's sympathy. As Zenchi had expected, his disciple advised him to try this method with such extraordinary urgency that, according to his premeditated plan, he finally yielded to his earnest counsel.

The formula was a simple one: first to boil the nose in hot water, and then to let another trample on it and torment it.

At the Temple bathhouse water was kept "at the boil" daily, so his disciple brought in an iron ladle, water so hot that no one could have put a finger into it. It was feared that Zenchi's face would be scalded by steam; so they bored a hole in a wooden tray and used the tray as a lid to cover the pot so that his nose could be immersed in the boiling water. As for his nose, no matter how long it was soaked in the scalding water, it was immune from ill effect.

"Your Reverence," the disciple said after a while, "I suppose it must be sufficiently boiled by now."

The Chaplain, with a wry smile, was thinking that no one who overheard this remark could suspect that it concerned a remedy for shortening his nose.

Heated by water and steam, his nose itched as if bitten by mosquitoes.

When the nose was withdrawn from the hole in the lid, the disciple set about trampling on that steaming object, exerting all his strength in pounding it with both his feet. Zenchi, lying on his side, and stretching his nose on the floorboards, watched his disciple's legs move up and down.

"Does it hurt, Your Reverence?" his disciple asked from time to time, looking down sympathetically on the priest's bald head. "The physician told me to trample hard on it. Doesn't it hurt?"

Zenchi tried to shake his head by way of indicating that he was not feeling any pain, but as his nose was being trampled on he could not do this, so rolling his eyes upwards, in a tone that suggested he was offended, and with his gaze fixed on his disciple's chapped feet, he said, "No, it doesn't hurt." Although his itching nose was being trampled on, it was a comfortable rather than a painful sensation.

His nose having undergone this treatment for some time, what seemed to be grains of millet began to appear, at which sight his disciple stopped trampling and said in soliloquy, "I was told to pull them out with tweezers."

The nose looked like a plucked and roasted chicken. With cheeks puffed out, though disgruntled, the priest suffered his disciple to deal with his nose as the man saw fit—although, however aware of his disciple's kindness he might have been, he did not relish his nose being treated as if it were a piece of inert matter. Like a patient undergoing an operation at the hands of a surgeon in whom he does not place implicit trust, Zenchi reluctantly watched his disciple extract, from the pores of his nose, feathers of fat curled to half an inch in diameter. The treatment finished, the disciple looked relieved and said: "Now, your Reverence, we have only to boil it once more, and it'll be all right."

Zenchi, with knit brow, submitted to the treatment meted out to him.

When his nose was taken out of the pot for the second time, it was found, to their great surprise, remarkably shorter than before and was not very different from a normal hooked nose. Stroking his greatly shortened nose, he timidly and nervously peered into the mirror which his disciple held out to him.

The nose, which previously had dangled below his chin, had miraculously dwindled, and, not protruding below his upper lip, was barely a relic of what it had once been. The red blotches

which bespeckled it were probably only bruises caused by the trampling.

"No one will laugh at me any more," the priest thought to himself. He saw in the mirror that the face reflected there was looking into the face outside the mirror, blinking its eyes in satisfaction.

But all day long he was uneasy and feared that his nose might grow long; so whenever he had the chance, whether in chanting sutras or in eating meals, he stealthily touched his nose. However, he found his nose installed in good shape above his upper lip, without straying beyond his lower lip.

Early in the morning, at the moment of waking, he stroked the tip of his nose, and he found that it was still as short as ever. After a gap of many years he at that moment recognized the same relief he had felt when he had completed the austerities required for his transcription of the lengthy Lotus Sutra of his sect.

Within the course of several days, however, Zenchi had a most surprising experience. A samurai who, on business, visited the Temple of Ike-no-O, looked amused as never before, and, quite incapable of uttering a word, he could but stare fixedly at the priest's nose. This was not all. The page who once had dropped Zenchi's nose into the bowl of gruel happened to pass by Zenchi in the lecture hall; at first, resisting his impulse to laugh, casting down his eyes, he could not for long withhold his burst of laughter. The sextons under Zenchi's supervision would listen respectfully while seated face to face with their master, but on more than one occasion they fell to chuckling as soon as he turned his back.

Zenchi at first attributed the laughter of his page and the sextons to the marked change in his features, but by and by, with his head cocked on one side, interrupting the sutra he was chanting, he would mutter to himself: "The change alone does not give a plausible explanation for their laughter. Zenchi Naigu! their laughter is now different from what it was when your nose was long. If you could say that the unfamiliar nose looks more ridiculous than the familiar one, that would once and for all settle the matter. But there must be some other reason behind it; they didn't laugh heartily or irresistibly as before."

The poor amiable priest on such occasions would look up at Fugen, Goddess of Wisdom, pictured on the scroll hanging close beside him, and calling to mind the long nose he had wielded until four or five days previously, he would lapse into melan-

choly "like one sunken low recalleth his glory of bygone days."
But it was to be regretted that he was deficient in judgment sufficient to find a solution to this quandary.

Man is possessed of two contradictory sentiments. Everyone will sympathize with another's misfortune. But when the other manages to pull through his misfortune, he not only thinks it safe to laugh at him to his face but also comes even to regard him with envy. In extreme cases some may feel like casting him into his former misfortune again and may even harbor some enmity, if negative, toward him.

Zenchi was at a loss to know what precisely made him forlorn, but his unhappiness was caused by nothing more than the wayward caprices of those surrounding him—the priests and laymen of Ike-no-O.

Day after day Zenchi, becoming more and more unhappy and vexed, would not open his mouth without speaking sharply to someone and was ever out-of-sorts until even the disciple who had administered to him the effective remedy began to backbite him, saying, "The master will be punished for his sins."

What especially enraged Zenchi was the mischief played on him by the page. One day, hearing a dog yelping wildly, he casually looked outside and found the page, with a stick about two feet long in his hand, chasing a lean and shaggy dog and shouting: "Watch out there for your *nose!* Watch out or I'll hit your *nose.*" Snatching the wooden stick from the page's hand, the priest struck him sharply across the face; it was the very stick which had been used to hold up Zenchi's nose.

Finally Zenchi came to feel sorry and even resentful for having had his long nose shortened.

One night after sunset it happened that the wind seeming to have arisen suddenly, the noisy tinkling of the pagoda wind bells came to his cell. The cold, moreover, had so noticeably increased in severity that Zenchi could not go to sleep, try as he might; tossing and turning in his bed he became aware of an itching in his nose. Putting his hand to his nose he felt that it had become swollen as if with dropsy; it seemed feverish, too.

"It was so drastically shortened that I might have caught some disease," he muttered to himself, caressing his nose as reverently as he would if he were holding the offerings of incense and flowers to be dedicated at the altar.

On the following morning Zenchi as usual awoke early, and he noticed that the garden was as bright as if it were carpeted

with gold, because in the garden the ginkgo trees and horse chestnuts had overnight shed all their leaves; and the crest of the pagoda must have been encrusted with frost, for the nine copper rings of the spire were brightly shining in the still faint glimmer of the rising sun. Sitting on the veranda, the shutters already opened, he drew a deep breath, and at that same moment a certain feeling, the nature of which he had all but forgotten, came back to him.

Instinctively he put his hand to his nose, and what he touched was not the short nose that had been his the night before, but the former long nose that had dangled five or six inches over his lips; in one night, he found, his nose had grown as long as it had been previously, and this, for some reason, made him feel refreshed and as happy as he had felt in the first moments when his nose had been shortened.

"Nobody will laugh at me any more," he whispered to himself.

His long nose dangled in the autumn breeze of early morning.

By Any Other Name

Santha Rama Rau

AT the Anglo-Indian day school in Zorinabad to which my sister and I were sent when she was eight and I was five and a half, they changed our names. On the first day of school, a hot, windless morning of a north Indian September, we stood in the headmistress's study and she said, "Now you're the *new* girls. What are your names?"

My sister answered for us. "I am Premila, and she"—nodding in my direction—"is Santha."

The headmistress had been in India, I suppose, fifteen years or so, but she still smiled her helpless inability to cope with Indian names. Her rimless half-glasses glittered, and the precarious bun on the top of her head trembled as she shook her head. "Oh, my dears, those are much too hard for me. Suppose we give you pretty English names. Wouldn't that be more jolly? Let's see, now—Pamela for you, I think." She shrugged in a baffled way at my sister. "That's as close as I can get. And for *you*" she said to me, "how about Cynthia? Isn't that nice?"

My sister was always less easily intimidated than I was, and while she kept a stubborn silence, I said, "Thank you," in a very tiny voice.

We had been sent to that school because my father, among his responsibilities as an officer of the civil service, had a tour of duty to perform in the villages around that steamy little provincial town, where he had his headquarters at that time. He used to make his shorter inspection tours on horseback, and a week before, in the stale heat of a typically postmonsoon day, we had waved goodbye to him and a little procession—an assistant, a secretary, two bearers, and the man to look after the bedding rolls and luggage. They rode away through our large garden, still bright green from the rains, and we turned back into the twilight of the house and the sound of fans whispering in every room.

Up to then, my mother had refused to send Premila to school in the British-run establishments of that time, because, she used to say, "you can bury a dog's tail for seven years and it still comes out curly, and you can take a Britisher away from his home for a lifetime and he still remains insular." The examina-

tions and degrees from entirely Indian schools were not, in those days, considered valid. In my case, the question had never come up, and probably never would have come up if Mother's extraordinary good health had not broken down. For the first time in my life, she was not able to continue the lessons she had been giving us every morning. So our Hindi books were put away, the stories of the Lord Krishna as a little boy were left in midair, and we were sent to the Anglo-Indian school.

That first day at school is still, when I think of it, a remarkable one. At that age, if one's name is changed, one develops a curious form of dual personality. I remember having a certain detached and disbelieving concern in the actions of "Cynthia," but certainly no responsibility. Accordingly, I followed the thin, erect back of the headmistress down the veranda to my classroom feeling, at most, a passing interest in what was going to happen to me in this strange, new atmosphere of School.

The building was Indian in design, with wide verandas opening onto a central courtyard, but Indian verandas are usually whitewashed, with stone floors. These, in the tradition of British schools, were painted dark brown and had matting on the floors. It gave a feeling of extra intensity to the heat.

I suppose there were about a dozen Indian children in the school—which contained perhaps forty children in all—and four of them were in my class. They were all sitting at the back of the room, and I went to join them. I sat next to a small, solemn girl who didn't smile at me. She had long, glossy black braids and wore a cotton dress, but she still kept on her Indian jewelry—a gold chain around her neck, thin gold bracelets, and tiny ruby studs in her ears. Like most Indian children, she had a rim of black kohl around her eyes. The cotton dress should have looked strange, but all I could think of was that I should ask my mother if I couldn't wear a dress to school, too, instead of my Indian clothes.

I can't remember too much about the proceedings in class that day, except for the beginning. The teacher pointed to me and asked me to stand up. "Now, dear, tell the class your name."

I said nothing.

"Come along," she said, frowning slightly. "What's your name, dear?"

"I don't know," I said, finally.

The English children in the front of the class—there were

about eight or ten of them—giggled and twisted around in their chairs to look at me. I sat down quickly and opened my eyes very wide, hoping in that way to dry them off. The little girl with the braids put out her hand and very lightly touched my arm. She still didn't smile.

Most of that morning I was rather bored. I looked briefly at the children's drawings pinned to the wall, and then concentrated on a lizard clinging to the ledge of the high, barred window behind the teacher's head. Occasionally it would shoot out its long yellow tongue for a fly, and then it would rest, with its eyes closed and its belly palpitating, as though it were swallowing several times quickly. The lessons were mostly concerned with reading and writing and simple numbers—things that my mother had already taught me—and I paid very little attention. The teacher wrote on the easel blackboard words like "bat" and "cat," which seemed babyish to me; only "apple" was new and incomprehensible.

When it was time for the lunch recess, I followed the girl with braids out onto the veranda. There the children from the other classes were assembled. I saw Premila at once and ran over to her, as she had charge of our lunchbox. The children were all opening packages and sitting down to eat sandwiches. Premila and I were the only ones who had Indian food—thin wheat chapatties, some vegetable curry, and a bottle of buttermilk. Premila thrust half of it into my hand and whispered fiercely that I should go and sit with my class, because that was what the others seemed to be doing.

The enormous black eyes of the little Indian girl from my class looked at my food longingly, so I offered her some. But she only shook her head and plowed her way solemnly through her sandwiches.

I was very sleepy after lunch, because at home we always took a siesta. It was usually a pleasant time of day, with the bedroom darkened against the harsh afternoon sun, the drifting off into sleep with the sound of Mother's voice reading a story in one's mind, and, finally, the shrill, fussy voice of the ayah waking one for tea.

At school, we rested for a short time on low, folding cots on the veranda, and then we were expected to play games. During the hot part of the afternoon we played indoors, and after the shadows had begun to lengthen and the slight breeze of the evening had come up we moved outside to the wide courtyard.

I had never really grasped the system of competitive games. At home, whenever we played tag or guessing games, I was always allowed to "win"—"because," Mother used to tell Premila, "she is the youngest, and we have to allow for that." I had often heard her say it, and it seemed quite reasonable to me, but the result was that I had no clear idea of what "winning" meant.

When we played twos-and-threes that afternoon at school, in accordance with my training. I let one of the small English boys catch me, but was naturally rather puzzled when the other children did not return the courtesy. I ran about for what seemed like hours without ever catching anyone, until it was time for school to close. Much later I learned that my attitude was called "not being a good sport," and I stopped allowing myself to be caught, but it was not for years that I really learned the spirit of the thing.

When I saw our car come up to the school gate, I broke away from my classmates and rushed toward it yelling, "Ayah! Ayah!" It seemed like an eternity since I had seen her that morning—a wizened, affectionate figure in her white cotton sari, giving me dozens of urgent and useless instructions on how to be a good girl at school. Premila followed more sedately, and she told me on the way home never to do that again in front of the other children.

When we got home we went straight to Mother's high, white room to have tea with her, and I immediately climbed onto the bed and bounced gently up and down on the springs. Mother asked how we had liked our first day in school. I was so pleased to be home and to have left that peculiar Cynthia behind that I had nothing whatever to say about school, except to ask what "apple" meant. But Premila told Mother about the classes, and added that in her class they had weekly tests to see if they had learned their lessons well.

I asked, "What's a test?"

Premila said, "You're too small to have them. You won't have them in your class for donkey's years." She had learned the expression that day and was using it for the first time. We all laughed enormously at her wit. She also told Mother, in an aside, that we should take sandwiches to school the next day. Not, she said, that *she* minded. But they would be simpler for me to handle.

That whole lovely evening I didn't think about school at all. I sprinted barefoot across the lawns with my favorite playmate, the cook's son, to the stream at the end of the garden. We quar-

reled in our usual way, waded in the tepid water under the lime trees, and waited for the night to bring out the smell of the jasmine. I listened with fascination to his stories of ghosts and demons, until I was too frightened to cross the garden alone in the semidarkness. The ayah found me, shouted at the cook's son, scolded me, hurried me in to supper—it was an entirely usual, wonderful evening.

It was a week later, the day of Premila's first test, that our lives changed rather abruptly. I was sitting at the back of my class, in my usual inattentive way, only half listening to the teacher. I had started a rather guarded friendship with the girl with the braids, whose name turned out to be Nalini (Nancy in school). The three other Indian children were already fast friends. Even at that age it was apparent to all of us that friendship with the English or Anglo-Indian children was out of the question. Occasionally, during the class, my new friend and I would draw pictures and show them to each other secretly.

The door opened sharply and Premila marched in. At first, the teacher smiled at her in a kindly and encouraging way and said, "Now, you're little Cynthia's sister?"

Premila didn't even look at her. She stood with her feet planted firmly apart and her shoulders rigid, and addressed herself directly to me. "Get up," she said. "We're going home."

I didn't know what had happened, but I was aware that it was a crisis of some sort. I rose obediently and started to walk toward my sister.

"Bring your pencils and your notebook," she said.

I went back for them, and together we left the room. The teacher started to say something just as Premila closed the door, but we didn't wait to hear what it was.

In complete silence we left the school grounds and started to walk home. Then I asked Premila what the matter was. All she would say was "We're going home for good."

It was a very tiring walk for a child of five and a half, and I dragged along behind Premila with my pencils growing sticky in my hand. I can still remember looking at the dusty hedges, and the tangles of thorns in the ditches by the side of the road, smelling the faint fragrance from the eucalyptus trees and wondering whether we would ever reach home. Occasionally a horse-drawn tonga passed us, and the women, in their pink or green silks, stared at Premila and me trudging along on the side of the road. A few coolies and a line of women carrying baskets

of vegetables on their heads smiled at us. But it was nearing the hottest time of day, and the road was almost deserted. I walked more and more slowly, and shouted to Premila, from time to time, "Wait for me!" with increasing peevishness. She spoke to me only once, and that was to tell me to carry my notebook on my head, because of the sun.

When we got to our house the ayah was just taking a tray of lunch into Mother's room. She immediately started a long, worried questioning about what are you children doing back here at this hour of the day.

Mother looked very startled and very concerned, and asked Premila what had happened.

Premila said, "We had our test today, and She made me and the other Indians sit at the back of the room, with a desk between each one."

Mother said, "Why was that, darling?"

"She said it was because Indians cheat," Premila added. "So I don't think we should go back to that school."

Mother looked very distant, and was silent a long time. At last she said, "Of course not, darling." She sounded displeased.

We all shared the curry she was having for lunch, and afterward I was sent off to the beautifully familiar bedroom for my siesta. I could hear Mother and Premila talking through the open door.

Mother said, "Do you suppose she understood all that?"

Premila said, "I shouldn't think so. She's a baby."

Mother said, "Well, I hope it won't bother her."

Of course, they were both wrong. I understood it perfectly, and I remember it all very clearly. But I put it happily away, because it had all happened to a girl called Cynthia, and I never was really particularly interested in her.

from
Kaffir Boy

Mark Mathabane

THE seven o'clock bus for blacks to Johannesburg was jam-packed with men and women on their way to the white world to work. A huge sign above the driver's booth read:

AUTHORIZED TO CARRY ONLY 65 SEATED PASSENGERS,
AND 15 STANDING.

But there must have been close to a hundred perspiring people squeezed into the stuffy bus. People sat on top of one another; some were sandwiched in the narrow aisle between the rows of seats, and some crowded on the steps. I sat on Granny's lap, in the middle of the bus, by a large smudged window. As the bus droned past Alexandra's boundaries, I glued my eyes to the window, anticipating my first look at the white world. What I saw made me think I had just made a quantum leap into another galaxy. I couldn't stop asking questions.

"What are those?"

"Skyscrapers."

"Why do they reach all the way to the sky?"

"Because many white people live and work in them."

Seconds later. "Wow! look at all those nice houses, Granny! They're so big! Do many white people live and work there, too?"

"No, those are mansions. Each is owned by one family."

"By one family!" I cried in disbelief. Each mansion occupied an area about three times that of the yard I lived in, yet the latter was home for over twenty families.

"Yes," Granny said matter-of-factly. "Your grandpa, when he first came to Johannesburg, worked for one such family. The family was so rich they owned an airplane."

"Why are there so many cars in the white people's homes?"

"Because they like to have many cars."

"Those people dressed in white, what game are they playing?"

"The men are playing cricket. Master Smith plays that, too. The women are playing tennis. Mrs. Smith plays it, too, on Tuesday and Thursday."

Suddenly the bus screeched to a halt, and people crashed into each other. I was thrown into the back of the wooden seat in front of me. Smarting, I asked, "Why did the bus suddenly stop? I didn't see any robots."

"Look over there," Granny pointed. "White schoolchildren are crossing the road."

I gazed through the window and for the first time in my life saw white schoolchildren. I scrutinized them for any differences from black schoolchildren, aside from color. They were like little mannequins. The boys were neatly dressed in snow-white shirts, blazers with badges, preppy caps with badges, ties matching the badges, shiny black and brown shoes, worsted knee-high socks. The girls wore pleated gymdresses with badges, snow-white shirts, caps with badges, blazers with badges, ties matching badges, shining black and brown shoes. A few of the girls had pigtails. On the back of each boy and girl was slung a schoolbag; and each frail, milky-white arm had a wristwatch on it. It suddenly struck me that we didn't even own a clock; we had to rely on cocks for time.

The white schoolchildren were filing out of a large, red-brick building with many large windows, in front of which were beds of multicolored flowers. A tall black man wearing a traffic uniform, a whistle between his thick lips, stood in the middle of the paved road, one hand raised to stop traffic, the other holding a sign that read in English and Afrikaans:

CHILDREN CROSSING
STOP
KINDERS STAP OOR

None of this orderly and safe crossing of the street ever took place at my school; we had to dash across.

The red-brick building stood on a vast tract of land with immaculate lawns, athletic fields, swings, merry-go-rounds, an Olympic-sized swimming pool, tennis courts, and rows of brightly leafed trees. In the driveway leading to the entrance of the building, scores of yellow school buses were parked. Not even the best of tribal schools in Alexandra—in the whole of South Africa—came close to having such magnificent facilities. At our school we didn't even have a school bus.

Oh, how I envied the white schoolchildren, how I longed to attend schools like theirs.

Minutes after all the white schoolchildren were safely across, traffic moved. At the next bus stop, we got off, and crossed the street when the robot flashed green. As we walked along the pavement, headed for Granny's workplace, I clutched her long dress, afraid of letting go, lest I be swallowed by the tremendous din of cars zooming up and down and honking in the busy streets. I began feeling dizzy as my eyes darted from one wonder to the next.

There were so many new and fantastic things around me that I walked as if in a dream. As we continued down the road, I became increasingly conscious of the curious looks white people gave us, as if we were a pair of escaped monkeys. Occasionally, Granny and I had jump off the pavement to make way for *madams* and their poodles and English toy spaniels. By constantly throwing my eyes sideways, I accidentally bumped into a parking meter.

We went up a side street. "There is Mrs. Smith's house," Granny remarked as she led me up a long driveway of a beautiful villa-type house surrounded by a well-manicured lawn with several beds of colorful, sweet-smelling flowers and rosebushes. We went to a steel gate in the back of the yard, where Granny rang a bell.

"I'm here, madam," she shouted through the gate. Immediately a dog started barking from within; I trembled.

Granny calmed me. A door creaked open, and a high-pitched woman's voice called out, "I'm coming, Ellen. Quiet, Buster, you naughty dog, it's Ellen." The barking ceased. Presently the gate clicked open, and there appeared a short, slender white woman with silver hair and slightly drooping shoulders. She wore white slacks, a white sweater, white shoes, and a white visor.

"I was just getting ready to leave for tennis," she said to Granny; she had not yet seen me.

"Madam, guess who I have with me today," Granny said with the widest smile.

I appeared like a jack-in-the-box. "Oh, my, you finally brought him with you!" Mrs. Smith exclaimed.

Breaking into a wide smile, revealing gleaming teeth, several of which were made of gold, she continued, "My, what a big lad he is! What small ears!"—touching them playfully—"Is he really your grandson, Ellen?" The warmth in her voice somehow reduced my fears of her; her eyes shone with the same gentleness of the Catholic sisters at the clinic.

"Yes, madam," Granny said proudly; "this is the one I've been telling you about. This is the one who'll some day go to university, like Master Clyde, and take care of me."

"I believe you, Ellen," said Mrs. Smith. "He looks like a very smart pickaninny." Turning to me, she asked, "How old are you?"

"Eleven, madam, eleven," I said, with so wide a smile I thought my jaws would lock.

"He's a year younger than Master Clyde," Granny said, "though the master is much bigger."

"A little chubby, you mean," Mrs. Smith said with a smile. "If you knew how much the little master eats, Ellen; I'm afraid he'll soon turn into a piglet. Sometimes I regret not having had another child. With a sibling, Master Clyde might have turned out differently. As it is, he's so spoiled as an only child."

"Pickaninny has one brother and three sisters." Granny said of me, "and the fifth one is on the way."

"My God! What a large family!" Mrs. Smith exclaimed. "What's the pickaninny's name?"

Using pidgin English, I proceeded not only to give my name and surname, but also my grade in school, home address, tribal affiliation, name of school, principal and teacher—all in a feverish attempt to justify Granny's label of me as a "smart one."

Mrs. Smith was astounded. "What a clever, clever pickaninny!" She turned to a tall, lean black man with an expressionless face and slightly stooping shoulders, dressed in housekeeper's livery (khaki shirt and pants), who had just emerged from the house and who led a poodle on a leash, and said, "Did you hear that, Absalom? Bantu children are smart. Soon they'll be running the country." Absalom simply tortured out a grin and took the poodle for a walk, after receiving instructions to bring brandy, whisky, wine and gin from the bottle store. Granny remarked that I was a "clever pickaninny" because of all the toys, games and comic books I had received from Master Clyde. Mrs. Smith seemed extremely pleased to hear that.

Before Mrs. Smith left for tennis, she said, "Ellen, your breakfast is near the washing machine in the garage. I'll be back sometime this afternoon. Please see to it that the flowers near the pool are watered, and that the rosebushes near the front of the gate are trimmed."

After a breakfast of coffee and peanut butter-and-jam sandwiches, Granny took out her gardening tools from the shed, and

we started working. As the two of us went about the large yard, I raked leaves and watered the flowers; Granny weeded the lawn. Mrs. Smith's neighbor's children kept on casting curious glances over the fence. From the way they looked at me, it seemed they were seeing a black child for the first time in their lives.

At midday, despite a scorching sun, Granny, seemingly indefatigable, went about with impressive skill trimming the rosebushes as we talked about trees and flowers and how to best cultivate them.

"Someday I'll build a house as big and beautiful as Mrs. Smith's," I said to Granny. "And a garden just as big and beautiful."

"Then I'll be your gardener," Granny said with a smile.

Toward early afternoon Mrs. Smith returned. She called me to the car to remove several shopping bags from the back seat. She took her tennis rackets, closed the doors, then sighed, "Phew, what a tiring day. Don't ever play tennis," she said to me, "it's a killer."

"What's tennis, madam?" I asked.

"You don't know tennis?" she exclaimed. "What sports do you play?"

"Soccer, madam."

"Ugh, that dangerous sport. Soccer is too rough. You should try tennis someday. It's a gentlemen's sport. Wouldn't you like to be a gentleman?"

"I would like to be a gentleman, madam," I replied, even though I hadn't the faintest idea what constituted a gentleman.

"Do you have tennis courts in Alexandra?"

"Yes, madam." The stadium where I played soccer was adjacent to four ramshackle sand courts, used primarily by kitchen girls and kitchen boys on their day off.

"Then I'll see if I can find an old racket for you," she said.

As we were talking, a busload of white schoolchildren stopped in front of the house, and a young boy, with a mop of rebellious brown hair, alighted and ran up the driveway toward Mrs. Smith. After giving her a kiss, he turned and demanded, "Who is he, Mother?"

"That's Ellen's grandson. The one you've been giving all those comic books and toys to."

"What is he doing here?"

"He's visiting us."

"What for? I don't want him here."

"Why not, Clyde," Mrs. Smith said. "he's a nice pickaninny.

Ellen is always nice to you, isn't she?"—the boy nodded with pursed lips—"now be nice to her grandson. Now run along inside and Absalom will show you the things I bought you today."

"Did you get my new bicycle and roller skates?"

"Yes, they'll be delivered Saturday. Now run in and change, an have something to eat. Then maybe you can play with pickaninny."

"I don't play with Kaffirs," the white boy declared. "At school they say we shouldn't."

"Watch your filthy mouth, Clyde," Mrs. Smith said, flushing crimson. "I thought I told you a million times to leave all that rubbish about Kaffirs in the classroom. Ellen's people are not Kaffirs, you hear! They're Bantus. Now go in and do as I told you." Turning to Granny, pruning a rosebush nearby, Mrs. Smith said, in a voice of someone fighting a losing battle. "You know, Ellen, I simply don't understand why those damn uncivilized Boers from Pretoria teach children such things. What future does this country have if this goes on?"

"I agree *makulu,* madam," Granny said, wiping her sweaty brow with her forearm. "All children, black and white, are God's children, madam. The preacher at my church tells us the Bible says so. `Suffer little children to come unto me, and forbid them not; for of such is the kingdom of heaven,' the Bible says. Is that not so, madam? Do you believe in the words of the Bible, madam?"

"I'm afraid you're right, Ellen," Mrs. Smith said, somewhat touched. "Yes, I do believe in the Bible. That's why I cannot accept the laws of this country. We white people are hypocrites. We call ourselves Christians, yet our deeds make the Devil look like a saint. I sometimes wish I hadn't left England."

I was struck by the openness of the discussion between Granny and Mrs. Smith.

"You're not like most white people I've worked for, madam," Granny said. "Master and you are kind toward our people. You treat us like human beings."

Mrs. Smith didn't answer; she hurried back indoors. Shortly thereafter, Clyde emerged in a pair of denims and a T-shirt advertising a South African rock group. He called out to me. "Come here, pickaninny. My mother says I should show you around."

I went.

I followed him around as he showed me all the things his parents regularly bought him: toys, bicycles, go-carts, pinball ma-

chines, Ping-Pong tables, electric trains. I only half-listened: my mind was preoccupied with comparing my situation with his. I couldn't understand why he and his people had to have all the luxuries money can buy, while I and my people lived in abject poverty. Was it because they were whites and we were black? Were they better than we? I could not find the answers; yet I felt there was something wrong about white people having everything, and black people nothing.

We finally came to Clyde's playroom. The room was roughly the size of our house, and was elaborately decorated with posters, pennants of various white soccer and cricket teams, rock stars and photographs of Clyde in various stages of development. But what arrested my attention were the stacks of comic books on the floor, and the shelves and shelves of books. Never had I seen that many books in my life; even our school, with a student population of over two thousand, did not have half as many books. I was dazed.

Sensing that I was in awe of his magnificent library, Clyde said, "Do you have this many books in your playroom?"

"I don't have a playroom."

"You don't have a playroom," he said bug-eyed. "Can you read?" he smiled sinisterly. "Our boy Absalom can't. And he says black children aren't taught much English at school."

"I can read a little English," I said.

"I doubt if you can read any of my books. Here, read," he ordered, pulling one out of the shelves. The book was thick, looked formidable.

I nervously opened a page, toiled through a couple lines, encountering long words I could not pronounce, let alone understand their meaning. Shaking my head in embarrassment, I handed the book back, "I can't read this type of English."

"Then you must be retarded," Clyde laughed. Though he might have meant it in jest, my pride was deeply wounded. "This book is by William Shakespeare," he went on, waving it in my face, "the greatest English writer that ever lived. I could read it from cover to cover when I was half your age. But I don't blame you if you can't. My teachers tell us that Kaffirs can't read, speak, or write English like white people because they have smaller brains, which are already full of tribal things. My teachers say you're not people like us, because you belong to a jungle civilization. That's why you can't live or go to school with us, but can only be our servants."

"Stop saying that rubbish, you naughty boy," Mrs. Smith said angrily as she entered the room just in time to catch the tail end of her son's knowledge of black people's intelligence, as postulated by the doctrine of apartheid. "How many times have I told you that what your teachers say about black people is not true?"

"What do you know, Mama?" Clyde retorted impudently, "you're not a teacher. Besides, there are textbooks where it's so written."

"Still it's not true," insisted Mrs. Smith. "Everything that's in your books is not necessarily true, especially your history books about this country." Changing the subject, she said, "Show him your easy books, and then get your things ready so I can drive you over to your friend's birthday party." Clyde quickly ran down his long list of "easy" books: *The Three Musketeers, Treasure Island, David Copperfield*, the Hardy Boys series, the Sherlock Holmes series, *Tom Sawyer, Robinson Crusoe, The Swiss Family Robinson, The Hunchback of Notre Dame, Black Beauty, A Tale of Two Cities*, and so on. Oh, how I envied Clyde's collection of books. I would have given my life to own just a handful of them.

The remark that black people had smaller brains and were thus incapable of reading, speaking, or writing English like white people had so wounded my ego that I vowed that, whatever the cost, I would master English, that I would not rest till I could read, write and speak it just like any white man, if not better. Finally, I had something to aspire to.

Back with Granny, I told her to be on the lookout whenever Mrs. Smith junked any books. At the end of the day, as Granny and I prepared to leave, I was given a small box by Mrs. Smith.

"It's from Clyde," she said. "He's sorry that he treated you badly. He's promised not to do it again. I'll see to it he keeps his promise. Come and help Ellen in the garden whenever you can; that way you'll earn some pocket money."

The box contained a couple shirts, pants, and jerseys. Underneath the articles of clothing was a copy of *Treasure Island*.

To learn to express my thoughts and feelings effectively in English became my main goal in life. I saw command of the English language as the crucial key with which to unlock doors leading into that wonderful world of books revealed to me through the reading of Robert Louis Stevenson's gripping tale of buried treasure, mutiny on the high seas, one-legged seamen, and the old sea song that I could recite even in my dreams:

*Fifteen men on a dead man's chest
Yo-ho-ho, and a bottle of rum.*

My heart ached to explore more such worlds, to live them in the imagination in much the same way as I lived the folktales of my mother and grandmother. I reasoned that if I somehow kept improving my English and ingratiated Mrs. Smith by the fact, then possibly she would give me more books like *Treasure Island* each time Granny took me along. Alas, such trips were few and far between. I could not afford to skip school regularly; and besides, each trip did not yield a book. But I clung to my dream.

A million times I wondered why the sparse library at my tribal school did not carry books like *Treasure Island,* why most of the books we read had tribal points of view. I would ask teachers and would be told that under the Bantu Education law black children were supposed to acquire a solid foundation in tribal life, which would prepare them for a productive future in their respective homelands. In this way the dream of Dr. Verwoerd, prime minister of South Africa and the architect of Bantu Education, would be realized, for he insisted that "the native child must be taught subjects which will enable him to work with and among his own people; therefore there is no use misleading him by showing him the green pastures of European society, in which he is not allowed to graze. Bantu Education should not be used to create imitation whites."

How I cursed Dr. Verwoerd and his law for prescribing how I should feel and think. I started looking toward the Smiths to provide me with the books about a different reality. Each day Granny came back from work around five in the afternoon, I would be the first to meet her at the gate, always with the same question, "Any books for me today?" Many times there weren't any. Unable to read new English books on a regular basis, I reread the ones I had over and over again, till the pages became dogeared. With each reading each book took on new life, exposed new angles to the story, with the result that I was never bored.

My bleak vocabulary did not diminish my enthusiasm for reading. I constantly borrowed Mr. Brown's pocket-size dictionary to look up meanings of words, and would memorize them like arithmetic tables and write them in a small notebook. Sometimes I would read the dictionary. My pronunciation was appalling, but I had no way of finding out. I was amazed at the

number of words in the English language, at the fact that a word could have different shades of meaning, or that certain words looked and sounded alike and yet differed greatly in meaning. Would I ever be able to learn all that?

At the same time I was discovering the richness of the English language I began imitating how white people talked, in the hope of learning proper pronunciation. My efforts were often hilarious, but my determination increased with failure. I set myself the goal of learning at least two new English words a day.

Marriage Is a Private Affair

Chinua Achebe

"HAVE you written to your dad yet?" asked Nene one afternoon as she sat with Nnaemeka in her room at 16 Kasanga
Street, Lagos.

"No. I've been thinking about it. I think it's better to tell him
when I get home on leave!"

"But why? Your leave is such a long way off yet—six whole
weeks. He should be let into our happiness now."

Nnaemeka was silent for a while, and then began very slowly
as if he groped for his words: "I wish I were sure it would be
happiness to him."

"Of course it must," replied Nene, a little surprised. "Why
shouldn't it?"

"You have lived in Lagos all your life, and you know very little
about people in remote parts of the country."

"That's what you always say. But I don't believe anybody will
be so unlike other people that they will be unhappy when their
sons are engaged to marry."

"Yes. They are most unhappy if the engagement is not arranged
by them. In our case it's worse—you are not even an Ibo."

This was said so seriously and so bluntly that Nene could not
find speech immediately. In the cosmopolitan atmosphere of the
city it had always seemed to her something of a joke that a person's tribe could determine whom he married.

At last she said, "You don't really mean that he will object to
your marrying me simply on that account? I had always thought
you Ibos were kindly disposed to other people."

"So we are. But when it comes to marriage, well, it's not quite
so simple. And this," he added, "is not peculiar to the Ibos. If
your father were alive and lived in the heart of Ibibio-land he
would be exactly like my father."

"I don't know. But anyway, as your father is so fond of you,
I'm sure he will forgive you soon enough. Come on then, be a
good boy and send him a nice lovely letter . . . ."

"It would not be wise to break the news to him by writing. A
letter will bring it upon him with a shock. I'm quite sure about
that."

"All right, honey, suit yourself. You know your father."

As Nnaemeka walked home that evening he turned over in his mind the different ways of overcoming his father's opposition, especially now that he had gone and found a girl for him. He had thought of showing his letter to Nene but decided on second thoughts not to, at least for the moment. He read it again when he got home and couldn't help smiling to himself. He remembered Ugoye quite well, an Amazon of a girl who used to beat up all the boys, himself included, on the way to the stream, a complete dunce at school.

I have found a girl who will suit you admirably—Ugoye Nweke, the eldest daughter of our neighbour, Jacob Nweke. She has a proper Christian upbringing. When she stopped schooling some years ago her father (a man of sound judgment) sent her to live in the house of a pastor where she has received all the training a wife could need. Her Sunday School teacher has told me that she reads her Bible very fluently. I hope we shall begin negotiations when you come home in December.

On the second evening of his return from Lagos Nnaemeka sat with his father under a cassia tree. This was the old man's retreat where he went to read his Bible when the parching December sun had set and a fresh, reviving wind blew on the leaves.

"Father," began Nnaemeka suddenly, "I have come to ask forgiveness."

"Forgiveness? For what, my son?" he asked in amazement.

"It's about this marriage question."

"Which marriage question?"

"I can't—we must—I mean it is impossible for me to marry Nweke's daughter."

"Impossible? Why?" asked his father.

"I don't love her."

"Nobody said you did. Why should you?" he asked.

"Marriage today is different . . . ."

"Look here, my son," interrupted his father, "nothing is different. What one looks for in a wife are a good character and a Christian background."

Nnaemeka saw there was no hope along the present line of argument.

"Moreover," he said, "I am engaged to marry another girl who

has all of Ugoye's good qualities, and who . . . ."

His father did not believe his ears. "What did you say?" he asked slowly and disconcertingly.

"She is a good Christian," his son went on, "and a teacher in a Girls' School in Lagos."

"Teacher, did you say? If you consider that a qualification for a good wife I should like to point out to you, Emeka, that no Christian woman should teach. St. Paul in his letter to the Corinthians says that women should keep silence." He rose slowly from his seat and paced forwards and backwards. This was his pet subject, and he condemned vehemently those church leaders who encouraged women to teach in their schools. After he had spent his emotion on a long homily he at last came back to his son's engagement, in a seemingly milder tone.

"Whose daughter is she, anyway?"

"She is Nene Atang."

"What!" All the mildness was gone again. "Did you say Ne-neataga, what does that mean?"

"Nene Atang from Calabar. She is the only girl I can marry." This was a very rash reply and Nnaemeka expected the storm to burst. But it did not. His father merely walked away into his room. This was most unexpected and perplexed Nnaemeka. His father's silence was infinitely more menacing than a flood of threatening speech. That night the old man did not eat.

When he sent for Nnaemeka a day later he applied all possible ways of dissuasion. But the young man's heart was hardened, and his father eventually gave him up as lost.

"I owe it to you, my son, as a duty to show you what is right and what is wrong. Whoever put this idea into your head might as well have cut your throat. It is Satan's work." He waved his son away.

"You will change your mind, Father, when you know Nene."

"I shall never see her," was the reply. From that night the father scarcely spoke to his son. He did not, however, cease hoping that he would realize how serious was the danger he was heading for. Day and night he put him in his prayers.

Nnaemeka, for his own part, was very deeply affected by his father's grief. But he kept hoping that it would pass away. If it had occurred to him that never in the history of his people had a man married a woman who spoke a different tongue, he might have been less optimistic. "It has never been heard," was the ver-

dict of an old man speaking a few weeks later. In that short sentence he spoke for all of his people. This man had come with others to commiserate with Okeke when news went round about his son's behaviour. By that time the son had gone back to Lagos.

"It has never been heard," said the old man again with a sad shake of his head.

"What did Our Lord say?" asked another gentleman. "Sons shall rise against their Fathers; it is there in the Holy Book."

"It is the beginning of the end," said another.

The discussion thus tending to become theological, Madubogwu, a highly practical man, brought it down once more to the ordinary level.

"Have you thought of consulting a native doctor about your son?" he asked Nnaemeka's father.

"He isn't sick," was the reply.

"What is he then? The boy's mind is diseased and only a good herbalist can bring him back to his right senses. The medicine he requires is *Amalile,* the same that women apply with success to recapture their husband's straying affection."

"Madubogwu is right," said another gentleman. "This thing calls for medicine."

"I shall not call in a native doctor." Nnaemeka's father was known to be obstinately ahead of his more superstitious neighbours in these matters. "I will not be another Mrs. Ochuba. If my son wants to kill himself let him do it with his own hands. It is not for me to help him."

"But it was her fault," said Madubogwu. "She ought to have gone to an honest herbalist. She was a clever woman, nevertheless."

"She was a wicked murderess," said Jonathan who rarely argued with his neighbours because, he often said, they were incapable of reasoning. "The medicine was prepared for her husband, it was his name they called in its preparation and I am sure it would have been perfectly beneficial to him. It was wicked to put it into the herbalist's food, and say you were only trying it out."

Six months later, Nnaemeka was showing his young wife a short letter from his father:

It amazes me that you could be so unfeeling as to send me your wedding picture. I would have sent it back. But on further

thought I decided just to cut off your wife and send it back to you because I have nothing to do with her. How I wish that I had nothing to do with you either.

When Nene read through this letter and looked at the mutilated picture her eyes filled with tears, and she began to sob.

"Don't cry, my darling," said her husband. "He is essentially good-natured and will one day look more kindly on our marriage." But years passed and that one day did not come.

For eight years, Okeke would have nothing to do with his son, Nnaemeka. Only three times (when Nnaemeka asked to come home and spend his leave) did he write to him.

"I can't have you in my house," he replied on one occasion. "It can be of no interest to me where or how you spend your leave—or your life, for that matter."

The prejudice against Nnaemeka's marriage was not confined to his little village. In Lagos, especially among his people who worked there, it showed itself in a different way. Their women, when they met at their village meeting were not hostile to Nene. Rather, they paid her such excessive deference as to make her feel she was not one of them. But as time went on, Nene gradually broke through some of this prejudice and even began to make friends among them. Slowly and grudgingly they began to admit that she kept her home much better than most of them.

The story eventually got to the little village in the heart of the Ibo country that Nnaemeka and his young wife were a most happy couple. But his father was one of the few people who knew nothing about this. He always displayed so much temper whenever his son's name was mentioned that everyone avoided it in his presence. By a tremendous effort of will he had succeeded in pushing his son to the back of his mind. The strain had nearly killed him but he had persevered, and won.

Then one day he received a letter from Nene, and in spite of himself he began to glance through it perfunctorily until all of a sudden the expression on his face changed and he began to read more carefully.

. . . Our two sons, from the day they learnt that they have a grandfather, have insisted on being taken to him. I find it impossible to tell them that you will not see them. I implore you to allow Nnaemeka to bring them home for a short time during his leave next month. I shall remain here in Lagos . . .

The old man at once felt the resolution he had built up over so many years falling in. He was telling himself that he must not give in. He tried to steel his heart against all emotional appeals. It was a re-enactment of that other struggle. He leaned against a window and looked out. The sky was overcast with heavy black clouds and a high wind began to blow filling the air with dust and dry leaves. It was one of those rare occasions when even Nature takes a hand in a human fight. Very soon it began to rain, the first rain in the year. It came down in large sharp drops and was accompanied by the lightning and thunder which mark a change of season. Okeke was trying hard not to think of his two grandsons. But he knew he was now fighting a losing battle. He tried to hum a favourite hymn but the pattering of large rain drops on the roof broke up the tune. His mind immediately returned to the children. How could he shut his door against them? By a curious mental process he imagined them standing, sad and forsaken, under the harsh angry weather—shut out from his house.

That night he hardly slept, from remorse—and a vague fear that he might die without making it up to them.

Telephone Conversation

Wole Soyinka

The price seemed reasonable, location
Indifferent. The landlady swore she lived
Off premises. Nothing remained
But self-confession. "Madam," I warned,
"I hate a wasted journey—I am African."
Silence. Silenced transmission of
Pressurized good breeding. Voice, when it came,
Lipstick-coated, long gold-rolled
Cigarette-holder pipped. Caught I was, foully.

"HOW DARK?" . . . . I had not misheard . . . "ARE YOU LIGHT
OR VERY DARK?" Button B. Button A. Stench
Of rancid breath of public hide-and-speak.
Red booth. Red pillar box. Red double-tiered
Omnibus squelching tar. It *was* real! Shamed
By ill-mannered silence, surrender
Pushed dumbfoundment to beg simplificaiton.
Considerate she was, varying the emphasis—

"ARE YOU DARK? OR VERY LIGHT?" Revelation came.
"You mean—like plain or milk chocolate?"
Her assent was clinical, crushing in its light
Impersonality. Rapidly, wave length adjusted,
I chose, "West African sepia"—and as an afterthought,
"Down in my passport." Silence for spectroscopic
Flight of fancy, till truthfulness clanged her accent
Hard on the mouthpiece "WHAT'S THAT?" conceding,
"DON'T KNOW WHAT THAT IS." "Like brunette."
"THAT'S DARK, ISN'T IT?" "Not altogether.

Facially, I am brunette, but madam, you should see
The rest of me. Palm of my hand, soles of my feet
Are a peroxide blonde. Friction, caused—
Foolishly, madam—by sitting down, has turned
My bottom raven black—One moment madam!"—sensing
Her receiver rearing on the thunder clap
About my ears—"Madam," I pleaded, "wouldn't you rather
See for yourself?"

A Sunrise on the Veld

Doris Lessing

EVERY night that winter he said aloud into the dark of the pillow: Half-past four! Half-past four! till he felt his brain had gripped the words and held them fast. Then he fell asleep at once, as if a shutter had fallen; and lay with his face turned to the clock so that he could see it first thing when he woke.

It was half-past four to the minute, every morning. Triumphantly pressing down the alarm-knob of the clock, which the dark half of his mind had outwitted, remaining vigilant all night and counting the hours as he lay relaxed in sleep, he huddled down for a last warm moment under the clothes, playing with the idea of lying abed for this once only. But he played with it for the fun of knowing that it was a weakness he could defeat without effort; just as he set the alarm each night for the delight of the moment when he woke and stretched his limbs, feeling the muscles tighten, and thought: Even my brain—even that! I can control every part of myself.

Luxury of warm rested body, with the arms and legs and fingers waiting like soldiers for a word of command! Joy of knowing that the precious hours were given to sleep voluntarily!—for he had once stayed awake three nights running, to prove that he could, and then worked all day, refusing even to admit that he was tired; and now sleep seemed to him a servant to be commanded and refused.

The boy stretched his frame full-length, touching the wall at his head with his hands, and the bedfoot with his toes; then he sprung out, like a fish leaping from water. And it was cold, cold.

He always dressed rapidly, so as to try and conserve his night-warmth till the sun rose two hours later; but by the time he had on his clothes his hands were numbed and he could scarcely hold his shoes. These he could not put on for fear of waking his parents, who never came to know how early he rose.

As soon as he stepped over the lintel, the flesh of his soles contracted on the chilled earth, and his legs began to ache with cold. It was night: the stars were glittering, the trees standing

black and still. He looked for signs of day, for the greying of the edge of a stone, or a lightening in the sky where the sun would rise, but there was nothing yet. Alert as an animal he crept past the dangerous window, standing poised with his hand on the sill for one proudly fastidious moment, looking in the stuffy blackness of the room where his parents lay.

Feeling for the grass-edge of the path with his toes, he reached inside another window further along the wall, where his gun had been set in readiness the night before. The steel was icy, and numbed fingers slipped along it, so that he had to hold it in the crook of his arm for safety. Then he tiptoed to the room where the dogs slept, and was fearful that they might have been tempted to go before him; but they were waiting, their haunches crouched in reluctance at the cold, but ears and swinging tails greeting the gun ecstatically. His warning undertone kept them secret and silent till the house was a hundred yards back: then they bolted off into the bush, yelping excitedly. The boy imagined his parents turning in their beds and muttering: Those dogs again! before they were dragged back in sleep; and he smiled scornfully. He always looked back over his shoulder at the house before he passed a wall of trees that shut it from sight. It looked so low and small, crouching there under a tall and brilliant sky. Then he turned his back on it, and on the frowsting sleepers, and forgot them.

He would have to hurry. Before the light grew strong he must be four miles away; and already a tint of green stood in the hollow of a leaf, and the air smelled of morning and the stars were dimming.

He slung the shoes over his shoulder, veld skoen that were crinkled and hard with the dews of a hundred mornings. They would be necessary when the ground became too hot to bear. Now he felt the chilled dust push up between his toes, and he let the muscles of his feet spread and settle into the shapes of the earth; and he thought: I could walk a hundred miles on feet like these! I could walk all day, and never tire!

He was walking swiftly through the dark tunnel of foliage that in day-time was a road. The dogs were invisibly ranging the lower travelways of the bush, and he heard then panting. Sometimes he felt a cold muzzle on his leg before they were off again, scouting for a trial to follow. They were not trained, but free-running companions of the hunt, who often tired of the long stalk before the final shots, and went off on their own pleasure.

Soon he could see them, small and wild-looking in a wild strange light, now that the bush stood trembling on the verge of colour, waiting for the sun to paint earth and grass afresh.

The grass stood to his shoulders; and the trees were showering a faint silvery rain. He was soaked; his whole body was clenched in a steady shiver.

Once he bent to the road that was newly scored with animal trails, and regretfully straightened, reminding himself that the pleasure of tracking must wait till another day.

He began to run along the edge of a field, noting jerkily how it was filmed over with fresh spiderweb, so that the long reaches of great black clods seemed netted in glistening grey. He was using the steady lope he had learned by watching the natives, the run that is a dropping of the weight of the body from one foot to the next in a slow balancing movement that never tires, nor shortens the breath; and he felt the blood pulsing down his legs and along his arms, and the exultation and pride of body mounted in him till he was shutting his teeth hard against a violent desire to shout his triumph.

Soon he had left the cultivated part of the farm. Behind him the bush was low and black. In front of a long vlei, acres of long pale grass that sent back a hollowing gleam of light to a satiny sky. Near him thick swathes of grass were bent with the weight of water, and diamond drops sparkled on each frond.

The first bird woke at is feet and at once a flock of them sprang into the air calling shrilly that day had come; and suddenly, behind him, the bush woke into song, and he could hear the guinea fowl calling far ahead of him. That meant they would now be sailing down from their trees into thick grass, and it was for them he had come: he was too late. But he did not mind. He forgot he had come to shoot. He set his legs wide, and balanced from foot to foot, and swung the gun up and down in both hands horizontally, in a kind of improvised exercise, and let his head sink back till it was pillowed in his neck muscles, and watched how above him small rosy clouds floated in a lake of gold.

Suddenly it all rose in him: it was unbearable. He leapt up into the air, shouting and yelling wild, unrecognisable noises. Then he began to run, not carefully, as he had before, but madly, like a wild thing. He was clean crazy, yelling mad with the joy of living and superfluity of youth. He rushed down the vlei under a tumult of crimson and gold, while all the birds of the world sang about him. He ran in great leaping strides, and

shouted as he ran, feeling his body rise into the crisp rushing air and fall back surely on to sure feet; and thought briefly, not believing that such a thing could happen to him, that he could break his ankle any moment, in this thick tangled grass. He cleared bushes like a duiker, leapt over rocks; and finally came to a dead stop at a place where the ground fell abruptly away below him to the river. It had been a two-mile-long dash through waist-high growth, and he was breathing hoarsely and could no longer sing. But he poised on a rock and looked down at stretches of water that gleamed through stooping trees, and thought suddenly, I am fifteen! Fifteen! The words came new to him; so that he kept repeating them wonderingly, with swelling excitement; and he felt the years of his life with is hands, as if he were counting marbles, each one hard and separate and compact, each one a wonderful shining thing. That was what he was: fifteen years of this rich soil, and this slow-moving water, and air that smelt like a challenge whether it was warm and sultry at noon, or brisk as cold water, like it was now.

There was nothing he couldn't do, nothing! A vision came to him, as he stood there, like when a child hears the word "eternity" and tries to understand it, and time takes possession of the mind. He felt his life ahead of him as a great and wonderful thing, something that was is; and he said aloud, with the blood rushing to his head: all the great men of the world have been as I am now, and there is nothing I can't become, nothing I can't do; there is no country in the world I cannot make part of myself, if I choose. I contain the world. I can make of it what I want. If I choose, I can change everything that is going to happen: it depends on me, and what I decide now.

The urgency and the truth and the courage of what his voice was saying exulted him so that he began to sing again, at the top of his voice, and the sound went echoing down the river gorge. He stopped for the echo, and sang again: stopped and shouted. That was what he was!—he sang, if he chose; and the world had to answer him.

And for minutes he stood there, shouting and singing and waiting for the lovely eddying sound of the echo; so that his own new strong thoughts came back and washed round his head, as if someone were answering him and encouraging him; till the gorge was full of soft voices clashing back and forth from rock to rock over the river. And then it seemed as if there was a new voice. He listened, puzzled, for it was not his own. Soon he was

leaning forward, all his nerves alert, quite still: somewhere close to him there was a noise that was no joyful bird, not tinkle of falling water, nor ponderous movement of cattle.

There it was again. In the deep morning hush that held his future and his past, was a sound of pain, and repeated over and over: it was a kind of shortened scream, as if someone, something, had no breath to scream. He came to himself, looked about him, and called for the dogs. They did not appear; they had gone off on their own business, and he was alone. Now he was clean sober, all the madness gone. His heart beating fast, because of that frightened screaming, he stepped carefully off the rock and went towards a belt of trees. He was moving cautiously, for not so long ago he had seen a leopard in just this spot.

At the edge of the trees he stopped and peered, holding his gun ready; he advanced, looking steadily about him, his eyes narrowed. Then all at once, in the middle of a step, he faltered, and his face was puzzled. He shook his head impatiently, as if he doubted his own sight.

There, between two trees, against a background of gaunt black rocks, was a figure from a dream, a strange beast that was horned and drunken-legged, but like something he had never even imagined. It seemed to be ragged. It looked like a small buck that had black ragged tufts of fur standing up irregularly all over it, with patches of raw flesh beneath . . . but the patches of rawness were disappearing under moving black and came again elsewhere; and all the time the creature screamed, in small gasping screams, and leaped drunkenly from side to side, as if it were blind.

Then the boy understood: it *was* a buck. He ran closer, and again stood still, stopped by a new fear. Around him the grass was whispering and alive. He looked wildly about, and then down. The ground was black with ants, great energetic ants that took no notice of him, but hurried and scurried towards the fighting shape, like glistening black water flowing through the grass.

And, as he drew in his breath and pity and terror seized him, the beast fell and the screaming stopped. Now he could hear nothing but one bird singing, and the sound of the rustling, whispering ants.

He peered over at the writhing blackness that jerked convulsively with the jerking nerves. It grew quieter. There were small twitches from the mass that still looked vaguely like the shape of a small animal.

It came into his mind that he should shoot it and end its pain; and he raised the gun. Then he lowered it again. The buck could not longer feel; its fighting was a mechanical protest of the nerves. But it was not that which made him put down the gun. It was a swelling feeling of rage and misery and protest that expressed itself in the thought: if I had not come it would have died like this: so why should I interfere? All over the bush things like this happen; they happen all the time; this is how life goes on, by living things dying in anguish. He gripped the gun between his knees and felt in his own limbs the myriad swarming pain of the twitching animal that could no longer feel, and set his teeth, and said over and over again under his breath: I can't stop it. I can't stop it. There is nothing I can do.

He was glad that the buck was unconscious and had gone past suffering so that he did not have to make a decision to kill it even when he was feeling with his whole body: this is what happens, this is how things work.

It was right—that was what he was feeling. *It was right and nothing could alter it.*

The knowledge of fatality, of what has to be, had gripped him and for the first time in his life; and he was left unable to make any movement of brain or body, except to say: "Yes, yes. That is what living is." It had entered his flesh and his bones and grown in to the furthest corners of his brain and would never leave him. And at that moment he could not have performed the smallest action of mercy, knowing as he did, having lived on it all his life, the vast unalterable, cruel veld, where at any moment one might stumble over a skull or crush the skeleton of some small creature.

Suffering, sick, and angry, but also grimly satisfied with his new stoicism, he stood there leaning on his rifle, and watched the seething black mound grow smaller. At his feet, now, were ants trickling back with pink fragments in their mouths, and there was a fresh acid smell in his nostrils. He sternly controlled the uselessly convulsing muscles of his empty stomach, and reminded himself: the ants must eat too! At the same time he found that the tears were streaming down his face, and his clothes were soaked with the sweat of that other creature's pain.

The shape had grown small. Now it looked like nothing recognisable. He did not know how long it was before he saw the blackness thin, and bits of white showed through, shining in the sun—yes, there was the sun, just up, glowing over the

rocks. Why, the whole thing could not have taken longer than a few minutes.

He began to swear, as if the shortness of the time was in itself unbearable, using the words he had heard his father say. He strode forward, crushing ants with each step, and brushing them off his clothes, till he stood above the skeleton, which lay sprawled under a small bush. It was clean-picked. It might have been lying there years, save that on the white bone were pink fragments of gristle. About the bones ants were ebbing away, their pincers full of meat.

The boy look at them, big black ugly insects. A few were standing and gazing up at him with small glittering eyes.

"Go away!" he said to the ants, very coldly. "I am not for you— not just yet, at any rate. Go away." And he fancied that the ants turned and went away.

He bent over the bones and touched the sockets in the skull, that was where the eyes were, he thought incredulously, re-membering the liquid dark eyes of a buck. And then he bent the slim foreleg bone, swinging it horizontally in his palm.

That morning, perhaps an hour ago, this small creature had been stepping proud and free through the bush, feeling the chill on its hide even as he himself had done, exhilarated by it. Proudly stepping the earth, tossing its horns, frisking a pretty white tail, it had sniffed the cold morning air. Walking like kings and conquerors it had moved through this free-held bush, where each blade of grass grew for it alone, and where the river ran pure sparking water for its slaking.

And then—what had happened? Such a swift surefooted thing could surely not be trapped by a swarm of ants?

The boy bent curiously to the skeleton. Then saw that the back leg that lay uppermost and strained out in the tension of death, was snapped midway in the thigh, so that broken bones jutted over each other uselessly. So that was it! Limping into the ant-masses it could not escape, once it had sensed the danger. Yes, but how had the leg been broken? Had it fallen, perhaps? Impossible, a buck was to light and graceful. Had some jealous rival horned it?

What could possibly have happened? Perhaps some Africans had thrown stones at it, as they do, trying to kill it for meat, and had broken its leg. Yes, that must be it.

Even as he imagined the crowd of running, shouting natives, and the flying stones, and the leaping buck, another picture

came into his mind. He saw himself, on any one of these bright ringing mornings, drunk with excitement, taking a snap shot at some half-seen buck. He saw himself with the gun lowered, wondering whether he had missed or not; and thinking at last that it was late, and he wanted his breakfast, and it was not worth while to track miles after an animal that would very likely get away from him in any case.

For a moment he would not face it. He was a small boy again, kicking sulkily at the skeleton, hanging his head, refusing to accept the responsibility.

Then he straightened up, and looked down at the bones with an odd expression of dismay, all the anger gone out him. His mind went quite empty; all around him he could see trickles of ants disappearing into the grass. The whispering noise was faint and dry, like the rustling of a cast snakeskin.

At last he picked up his gun and walked homewards. He was telling himself half defiantly that he wanted his breakfast. He was telling himself that it was getting very hot, much too hot to be out roaming the bush.

Really, he was tired. He walked heavily, not looking where he put his feet. When he came within sight of his home he stopped, knitting his brows. There was something he had to think out. The death of that small animal was a thing that concerned him, and he was by no means finished with it. It lay at the back of his mind uncomfortably.

Soon, the very next morning, he would get clear of everybody and go to the bush and think about it.

Seven Laments for the War-Dead

Yehuda Amichai

1
Mr. Beringer, whose son
fell at the Canal that strangers dug
so ships could cross the desert,
crosses my path at Jaffa Gate.

He has grown very thin, has lost
the weight of his son.
That's why he floats so lightly in the alleys
and gets caught in my heart like little twigs
that drift away.

2
As a child he would mash his potatoes
to a golden mush.
And then you die.

A living child must be cleaned
when he comes home from playing.
But for a dead man
earth and sand are clear water, in which
his body goes on being bathed and purified
forever.

3
The Tomb of the Unknown Soldier
across there. On the enemy's side. A good landmark
for gunners of the future.

Or the war monument in London
at Hyde Park Corner, decorated
like a magnificent cake: yet another soldier
lifting head and rifle,
another cannon, another eagle, another
stone angel.

And the whipped cream of a huge marble flag
poured over it all
with an expert hand.

But the candied, much-too-red cherries
were already gobbled up
by the glutton of hearts. Amen.

4
I came upon an old zoology textbook,
Brehm, Volume II, *Birds:*
in sweet phrases, an account of the life of the starling,
swallow, and thrush. Full of mistakes in an antiquated
Gothic typeface, but full of love, too. "Our feathered
friends." "Migrate from us to the warmer climes."
Nest, speckled egg, soft plumage, nightingale,
stork. "The harbingers of spring." The robin,
red-breasted.

Year of publication: 1913, Germany,
on the eve of the war that was to be
the eve of all my wars.

My good friend who died in my arms, in
his blood,
on the sands of Ashdod. 1948, June.

Oh my friend,
red-breasted.

5
Dicky was hit.
Like the water tower at Yad Mordekhai.
Hit. A hole in the belly. Everything
came flooding out.

But he has remained standing like that
in the landscape of my memory
like the water tower at Yad Mordekhai.

He fell not far from there,
a little to the north, near Houlayqat.

6

Is all of this
sorrow? I don't know.
I stood in the cemetery dressed in
the camouflage clothes of a living man: brown pants
and a shirt yellow as the sun.

Cemeteries are cheap; they don't ask for much.
Even the wastebaskets are small, made for holding
tissue paper
that wrapped flowers from the store.
Cemeteries are a polite and disciplined thing.
"I shall never forget you," in French
on a little ceramic plaque.
I don't know who it is that won't ever forget:
he's more anonymous than the one who died.

Is all of this sorrow? I guess so.
"May ye find consolation in the building
of the homeland." But how long
can you go on building the homeland
and not fall behind in the terrible
three-sided race
between consolation and building and death?

Yes, all of this sorrow. But leave
a little love burning always
like the small bulb in the room of a sleeping baby
that gives him a bit of security and quiet love
though he doesn't know what the light is
or where it comes from.

7

Memorial Day for the war-dead: go tack on
the grief of all your losses—
including a woman who left you—
to the grief of losing them; go mix
one sorrow with another, like history,
that in its economical way
heaps pain and feast and sacrifice
onto a single day for easy reference.

Oh sweet world, soaked like bread
in sweet milk for the terrible
toothless God. "Behind all this,
some great happiness is hiding." No use
crying inside and screaming outside.
Behind all this, some great happiness may
be hiding.

Memorial day. Bitter salt, dressed up as
a little girl with flowers.
Ropes are strung out the whole length of the route
for a joint parade: the living and the dead together.
Children move with the footsteps of someone else's grief
as if picking their way through broken glass.

The flautist's mouth will stay pursed fro many days.
A dead soldier swims among the small heads
with the swimming motions of the dead,
with the ancient error the dead have
about the place of the living water.

A flag loses contact with reality and flies away.
A store window decked out with beautiful dresses for
  women
in blue and white. And everything
in three languages: Hebrew, Arabic, and Death.

A great royal beast has been dying all night long
under the jasmine,
with a fixed stare at the world.
A man whose son died in the war
walks up the street
like a woman with a dead fetus in her womb.
"Behind all this, some great happiness is hiding."

Half a Day

Naguib Mahfouz

Translated by Denys Johnson-Davies

I proceeded alongside my father, clutching his right hand, running to keep up with the long strides he was taking. All my clothes were new: the black shoes, the green school uniform, and the red tarboosh. My delight in my new clothes, however, was not altogether unmarred, for this was no feast day but the day on which I was to be cast into school for the first time.

My mother stood at the window watching our progress, and I would turn toward her from time to time, as though appealing for help. We walked along a street lined with gardens; on both sides were extensive fields planted with crops, prickly pears, henna trees, and a few date palms.

"Why school?" I challenged my father openly. "I shall never do anything to annoy you."

"I'm not punishing you," he said, laughing. "School's not a punishment. It's the factory that makes useful men out of boys. Don't you want to be like your father and brothers?"

I was not convinced. I did not believe there was really any good to be had in tearing me away from the intimacy of my home and throwing me into this building that stood at the end of the road like some huge, high-walled fortress, exceedingly stern and grim.

When we arrived at the gate we could see the courtyard, vast and crammed full of boys and girls. "Go in by yourself," said my father, "and join them. Put a smile on your face and be a good example to others."

I hesitated and clung to his hand, but he gently pushed me from him. "Be a man," he said. "Today you truly begin life. You will find me waiting for you when it's time to leave."

I took a few steps, then stopped and looked but saw nothing. Then the faces of boys and girls came into view. I did not know a single one of them, and none of them knew me. I felt I was a stranger who had lost his way. But glances of curiosity were directed toward me, and one boy approached and asked, "Who brought you?"

"My father," I whispered.

"My father's dead," he said quite simply.

I did not know what to say. The gate was closed, letting out a pitiable screech. Some of the children burst into tears. The bell rang. A lady came along, followed by a group of men. The men began sorting us into ranks. We were formed into an intricate pattern in the great courtyard surrounded on three sides by high buildings of several floors; from each floor we were over-looked by a long balcony roofed in wood.

"This is your new home," said the woman. "Here, too, there are mothers and fathers. Here there is everything that is enjoy-able and beneficial to knowledge and religion. Dry your tears and face life joyfully."

We submitted to the facts, and this submission brought a sort of contentment. Living beings were drawn to other living beings, and from the first moments my heart made friends with such boys as were to be my friends and fell in love with such girls as I was to be in love with, so that it seemed my misgivings had had no basis. I had never imagined school would have this rich vari-ety. We played all sorts of different games: swings, the vaulting horse, ball games. In the music room we chanted our first songs. We also had our first introduction to language. We saw a globe of the Earth, which revolved and showed the various continents and countries. We started learning the numbers. The story of the Creator of the universe was read to us, we were told of His pre-sent world and of His Hereafter, and we heard examples of what He said. We ate delicious food, took a little nap, and woke up to go on with friendship and love, play and learning.

As our path revealed itself to us, however, we did not find it as totally sweet and unclouded as we had presumed. Dust-laden winds and unexpected accidents came about suddenly, so we had to be watchful, at the ready, and very patient. It was not all a matter of playing and fooling around. Rivalries could bring about pain and hatred or give rise to fighting. And while the lady would sometimes smile, she would often scowl and scold. Even more frequently she would resort to physical punishment.

In addition, the time for changing one's mind was over and gone and there was no question of ever returning to the par-adise of home. Nothing lay ahead of us but exertion, struggle, and perseverance. Those who were able took advantage of the opportunities for success and happiness that presented them-selves amid the worries.

The bell rang announcing the passing of the day and the end of work. The throngs of children rushed toward the gate, which was opened again. I bade farewell to friends and sweethearts

and passed through the gate. I peered around but found no trace of my father, who had promised to be there. I stepped aside to wait. When I had waited for a long time without avail, I decided to return home on my own. After I had taken a few steps, a middle-aged man passed by, and I realized at once that I knew him. He came toward me, smiling, and shook me by the hand, saying, "It's a long time since we last met—how are you?"

With a nod of my head, I agreed with him and in turn asked, "And you, how are you?"

"As you can see, not all that good, the Almighty be praised!"

Again he shook me by the hand and went off. I proceeded a few steps, then came to a startled halt. Good Lord! Where was the street lined with gardens? Where had it disappeared to? When did all these vehicles invade It? And when did all these hordes of humanity come to rest upon its surface? How did these hills of refuse come to cover its sides? And where were the fields that bordered it? High buildings had taken over, the street surged with children, and disturbing noises shook the air. At various points stood conjurers showing off their tricks and making snakes appear from baskets. The there was a band announcing the opening of a circus, with clowns and weight lifters walking in front. A line of trucks carrying central security troops crawled majestically by. The siren of a fire engine shrieked, and it was not clear how the vehicle would cleave its way to reach the blazing fire. A battle raged between a taxi driver and his passenger, while the passenger's wife called out for help and no one answered. Good God! I was in a daze. My head spun. I almost went crazy. How could all this have happened in half a day, between early morning and sunset? I would find the answer at home with my father. But where was my home? I could see only tall buildings and hordes of people. I hastened on to the crossroads between the gardens and Abu Khoda. I had to cross Abu Khoda to reach my house, but the stream of cars would not let up. The fire engine's siren was shrieking at full pitch as it moved at a snail's pace, and I said to myself, "Let the fire take its pleasure in what it consumes." Extremely irritated, I wondered when I would be able to cross. I stood there a long time, until the young lad employed at the ironing shop on the corner came up to me. He stretched out his arm and said gallantly, "Grandpa, let me take you across."

Axolotl

Julio Cortázar

Translated by Paul Blackburn

THERE was time when I thought a great deal about the axolotls. I went to see them in the aquarium at the Jardin des
Plantes and stayed for hours watching them, observing their immobility, their faint movements. Now I am an axolotl.

I got to them by chance one spring morning when Paris was
spreading its peacock tail after a wintry Lent. I was heading
down the boulevard Port-Royal, then I took Saint-Marcel and
L'Hôpital and saw green among all that gray and remembered
the lions. I was friend of the lions and panthers, but had never
gone into the dark, humid building that was the aquarium. I left
my bike against the gratings and went to look at the tulips. The
lions were sad and ugly and my panther was asleep. I decided
on the aquarium, looked obliquely at banal fish until, unexpectedly, I hit it off with the axolotls. I stayed watching them for an
hour and left, unable to think of anything else.

In the library at Sainte-Geneviève, I consulted a dictionary
and learned that axolotls are the larval stage (provided with
gills) of a species of salamander of the genus *Ambystoma*. That
they were Mexican I knew already by looking at them and their
little pink Aztec faces and the placard at the top of the tank. I
read that specimens of them had been found in Africa capable
of living on dry land during the periods of drought, and continuing their life under water when the rainy season came. I found
their Spanish name, *ajolote,* and the mention that they were ed-
ible, and that their oil was used (no longer used, it said) like
cod-liver oil.

I didn't care to look up any of the specialized works, but the
next day I went back to the Jardin des Plantes. I began to go
every morning, morning and afternoon some days. The aquarium guard smiled perplexedly, taking my ticket. I would lean up
against the iron bar in front of the tanks and set to watching
them. There's nothing strange in this, because after the first
minute I knew that we were linked, that something infinitely lost
and distant kept pulling us together. It had been enough to de-
tain me that first morning in front of the sheet of glass where

some bubbles rose through the water. The axolotls huddled on the wretched narrow (only I can know how narrow and wretched) floor of moss and stone in the tank. There were nine specimens, and the majority pressed their heads against the glass, looking with their eyes of gold at whoever came near them. Disconcerted, almost ashamed, I felt it a lewdness to be peering at these silent and immobile figures heaped at the bottom of the tank. Mentally I isolated one, situated on the right and somewhat apart from the others, to study it better. I saw a rosy little body, translucent (I thought of those Chinese figurines of milky glass), looking like a small lizard about six inches long, ending in a fish's tail of extraordinary delicacy, the most sensitive part of our body. Along the back ran a transparent fin which joined with the tail, but what obsessed me was the feet, of the slenderest nicety, ending in tiny fingers with minutely human nails. And then I discovered its eyes, its face. Inexpressive features, with no other trait save the eyes, two orifices, like brooches, wholly of transparent gold, lacking any life but looking, letting themselves be penetrated by my look, which seemed to travel past the golden level and lose itself in a diaphanous interior mystery. A very slender black halo ringed the eye and etched it onto the pink flesh, onto the rosy stone of the head, vaguely triangular, but with curved and irregular sides which gave it a total likeness to a statuette corroded by time. The mouth was masked by the triangular plane of the face, its considerable size would be guessed only in profile; in front of a delicate crevice barely slit the lifeless stone. On both sides of the head where the ears should have been, there grew three tiny sprigs red as coral, a vegetal outgrowth, the gills, I suppose. And they were the only thing quick about it; every ten or fifteen seconds the sprigs pricked up stiffly and again subsided. Once in a while a foot would barely move, I saw the diminutive toes poise mildly on the moss. It's that we don't enjoy moving a lot, and the tank is so cramped—we barely move in any direction and we're hitting one of the others with our tail or our head—difficulties arise, fights, tiredness. The time feels like it's less if we stay quietly.

It was their quietness that made me lean toward them fascinated the first time I saw the axolotls. Obscurely I seemed to understand their secret will, to abolish space and time with an indifferent immobility. I knew better later; the gill contraction, the tentative reckoning of the delicate feet on the stones, the abrupt swimming (some of them swim with a simple undulation

of the body) proved to me that they were capable of escaping that mineral lethargy in which they spent whole hours. Above all else, their eyes obsessed me. In the standing tanks on either side of them, different fishes showed me the simple stupidity of their handsome eyes so similar to our own. The eyes of the axolotls spoke to me of the presence of a different life, of another way of seeing. Gluing my face to the glass (the guard would cough fussily once in a while), I tried to see better those diminutive golden points, that entrance to the infinitely slow and remote world of these rosy creatures. It was useless to tap with one finger on the glass directly in front of their faces; they never gave the least reaction. The golden eyes continued burning with their soft, terrible light; they continued looking at me from an unfathomable depth which made me dizzy.

And nevertheless they were close. I knew it before this, before being an anxolotl. I learned it the day I came near them for the first time. The anthropomorphic features of a monkey reveal the reverse of what most people believe, the distance that is traveled from them to us. The absolute lack of similarity between axolotls and human beings proved to me that my recognition was valid, that I was not propping myself up with easy analogies. Only the little hands . . . But an eft, the common newt, has such hands also, and we are not at all alike. I think it was the axolotls' heads, that triangular pink shape with the tiny eyes of gold. That looked and knew. That laid the claim. They were not *animals*.

It would seem easy, almost obvious, to fall into mythology. I began seeing in the axolotls a metamorphosis which did not succeed in revoking a mysterious humanity. I imagined them aware, slaves of their bodies, condemned infinitely to the silence of the abyss, to a hopeless meditation. Their blind gaze, the diminutive gold disk without expression and nonetheless terribly shining, went through me like a message: "Save us, save us." I caught myself mumbling words of advice, conveying childish hopes. They continued to look at me, immobile; from time to time the rosy branches of the gills stiffened. In that instant I felt a muted pain; perhaps they were seeing me, attracting my strength to penetrate into the impenetrable thing of their lives. They were not human beings, but I had found in no animal such a profound relation with myself. The axolotls were like witnesses of something, and at times like horrible judges. I felt ignoble in front of them; there was such a terrifying purity in those transparent eyes. They were larvas, but larva means disguise and also

phantom. Behind those Aztec faces, without expression but of an implacable cruelty, what semblance was awaiting its hour?

I was afraid of them. I think that had it not been for feeling the proximity of other visitors and the guard, I would not have been bold enough to remain alone with them. "You eat them alive with your eyes, hey," the guard said, laughing; he likely thought I was a little cracked. What he didn't notice was that it was they devouring me slowly with their eyes, in a cannibalism of gold. At any distance from the aquarium, I had only to think of them, it was as though I were being affected from a distance. It got to the point that I was going every day, and at night I thought of them immobile in the darkness, slowly putting a hand out which immediately encountered another. Perhaps their eyes could see in the dead of night, and for them the day continued indefinitely. The eyes of axolotls have no lids.

I know now that there was nothing strange, that that had to occur. Leaning over in front of the tank each morning, the recognition was greater. They were suffering, every fiber of my body reached toward that stifled pain, that stiff torment at the bottom of the tank. They were lying in wait for something, a remote dominion destroyed, an age of liberty when the world had been that of the axolotls. Not possible that such a terrible expression which was attaining the overthrow of that forced blankness on their stone faces should carry any message other than one of pain, proof of that eternal sentence, of that liquid hell they were undergoing. Hopelessly, I wanted to prove to myself that my own sensibility was projecting a nonexistent consciousness upon the axolotls. They and I knew. So there was nothing strange in what happened. My face was pressed against the glass of the aquarium, my eyes were attempting once more to penetrate the mystery of those eyes of gold without iris, without pupil. I saw from very close up the face of an axolotl immobile next to the glass. No transition and no surprise, I saw my face against the glass, I saw it on the outside of the tank, I saw it on the other side of the glass. Then my face drew back and I understood.

Only one thing was strange: to go on thinking as usual, to know. To realize that was, for the first moment, like the horror of a man buried alive awakening to his fate. Outside, my face came close to the glass again, I saw my mouth, the lips compressed with the effort of understanding the axolotls. I was an axolotl and now I knew instantly that no understanding was possible. He was outside the aquarium, his thinking was a thinking out-

side the tank. Recognizing him, being him himself, I was an axolotl and in my world. The horror began—I learned in the same moment—of believing myself prisoner in the body of an axolotl, metamorphosed into him with my human mind intact, buried alive in an axolotl, condemned to move lucidly among unconscious creatures. But that stopped when a foot just grazed my face, when I moved just a little to one side and saw an axolotl next to me who was looking at me, and understood that he knew also, no communication possible, but very clearly. Or I was also in him, or all of us were thinking humanlike, incapable of expression, limited to the golden splendor of our eyes looking at the face of the man pressed against the aquarium.

He returned many times, but he comes less often now. Weeks pass without his showing up. I saw him yesterday, he looked at me for a long time and left briskly. It seemed to me that he was not so much interested in us any more, that he was coming out of habit. Since the only thing I do is think, I could think about him a lot. It occurs to me that at the beginning we continued to communicate, that he felt more than ever one with the mystery which was claiming him. But the bridges were broken between him and me, because what was his obsession is now an axolotl, alien to his human life. I think that at the beginning I was capable of returning to him in a certain way—ah, only in a certain way—and of keeping awake his desire to know us better. I am an axolotl for good now, and if I think like a man it's only because every axolotl thinks like a man inside his rosy stone semblance. I believe that all this succeeded in communicating something to him in those first days, when I was still he. And in this final solitude to which he no longer comes, I console myself by thinking that perhaps he is going to write a story about us, that, believing he's making up a story, he's going to write all this about axolotls.

Serene Words

Gabriela Mistral

Now in the middle of my days I glean
this truth that has a flower's freshness:
life is the gold and sweetness of wheat,
hate is brief and love immense.

Let us exchange for a smiling verse
that verse scored with blood and gall.
Heavenly violets open, and through the valley
the wind blows a honeyed breath.

Now I understand not only the man who prays;
now I understand the man who breaks into song.
Thirst is long-lasting and the hillside twisting;
but a lily can ensnare our gaze.

Our eyes grow heavy with weeping,
yet a brook can make us smile.
A skylark's song bursting heavenward
makes us forget it is hard to die.

There is nothing now that can pierce my flesh.
With love, all turmoil ceased.
The gaze of my mother still brings me peace.
I fee that God is putting me to sleep.

Wind and Water and Stone

Octavio Paz

Translated by Mark Strand

for Roger Caillois
The water hollowed the stone,
the wind dispersed the water,
the stone stopped the wind.
Water and wind and stone.

The wind sculpted the stone,
the stone is a cup of water,
the water runs off and is wind.
Stone and wind and water.

The wind sings in its turnings,
the water murmurs as it goes,
the motionless stone is quiet.
Wind and water and stone.

One is the other, and is neither:
among their empty names
they pass and disappear,
water and stone and wind.

The Garden of Forking Paths

Jorge Luis Borges

Translated by Donald A. Yates

ON page 22 of Liddell Hart's *History of World War I* you will read that an attack against the Serre-Montauban line by thirteen British divisions (supported by 1,400 artillery pieces), planned for the 24th of July, 1916, had to be postponed until the morning of the 29th. The torrential rains, Captain Liddell Hart comments, caused this delay, an insignificant one, to be sure.

The following statement, dictated, reread and signed by Dr. Yu Tsun, former professor of English at the *Hochschule* at Tsingtao, throws an unsuspected light over the whole affair. The first two pages of the document are missing.

". . . and I hung up the receiver. Immediately afterwards, I recognized the voice that had answered in German. It was that of Captain Richard Madden. Madden's presence in Viktor Runeberg's apartment mean the end of our anxieties and—but this seemed, *or should have seemed,* very secondary to me—also the end of our lives. It meant that Runeberg had been arrested or murdered. Before the sun set on that day, I would encounter the same fate. Madden was implacable. Or rather, he was obliged to be so. An Irishman at the service of England, a man accused of laxity and perhaps of treason, how could he fail to seize and be thankful for such a miraculous opportunity: the discovery, capture, maybe even the death of two agents of the German Reich? I went up to my room; absurdly I locked the door and threw myself on my back on the narrow iron cot. Through the window I saw the familiar roofs and the cloud-shaded six o'clock sun. It seemed incredible to me that that day without premonitions or symbols should be the one of my inexorable death. In spite of my dead father, in spite of having been a child in a symmetrical garden of Hai Feng, was I—now—going to die? Then I reflected that everything happens to a man precisely, precisely now. Centuries of centuries and only in the present do things happen; countless men in the air, on the face of the earth and the sea, and all that really is happening is happening to me . . . The almost intolerable recollection of Madden's horselike face banished these wanderings. In the midst of my hatred and terror (it means nothing to me

now to speak of terror, now that I have mocked Richard Madden, now that my throat yearns for the noose) it occurred to me that the tumultuous and doubtless happy warrior did not suspect that I possessed the Secret. The name of the exact location of the new British artillery park on the River Ancre. A bird streaked across the gray sky and blindly I translated it into an airplane and that airplane into many (against the French sky) annihilating the artillery station with vertical bombs. If only my mouth, before a bullet shattered it, could cry out that secret name so it could be heard in Germany . . . My human voice was very weak. How might I make it carry to the ear of the Chief? To the ear of that sick and hateful man who knew nothing of Runeberg and me save that we were in Staffordshire and who was waiting in vain for our report in his arid office in Berlin, endlessly examining newspapers . . . I said out loud: *I must flee.* I sat up noiselessly, in a useless perfection of silence, as if Madden were already lying in wait for me. Something—perhaps the mere vain ostentation of proving my resources were nil—made me look through my pockets. I found what I knew I would find. The American watch, the nickel chain and the square coin, the key ring with the incriminating useless keys to Runeberg's apartment, the notebook, a letter which I resolved to destroy immediately (and which I did not destroy), a crown, two shillings and few pence, the red and blue pencil, the handkerchief, the revolver with one bullet. Absurdly, I took it in my hand and weighed it in order to inspire courage within myself. Vaguely I thought that a pistol report can be heard at a great distance. In ten minutes my plan was perfected. The telephone book listed the name of the only person capable of transmitting the message; he lived in a suburb of Fenton, less than a half hour's train ride away.

I am a cowardly man. I say it now, now that I have carried to its end a plan whose perilous nature no one can deny. I know its execution was terrible. I didn't do it for Germany, no. I care nothing for a barbarous country which imposed upon me the abjection of being a spy. Besides, I know of a man from England—a modest man—who for me is no less great than Goethe. I talked with him for scarcely an hour, but during that hour he was Goethe . . . I did it because I sensed that the Chief somehow feared people of my race—for the innumerable ancestors who merge within me. I wanted to prove to him that a yellow man could save his armies. Besides, I had to flee from Captain Madden. His hands and his voice could call at my door at any moment. I dressed silently, bade farewell to myself in the mirror,

went downstairs, scrutinized the peaceful street and went out. The station was not far from my home, but I judged it wise to take a cab. I argued that in this way I ran less risk of being recognized; the fact is that in the deserted street I felt myself visible and vulnerable, infinitely so. I remember that I told the cab driver to stop a short distance before the main entrance. I got out with voluntary, almost painful slowness; I was going to the village of Ashgrove but I bought a ticket for a more distant station. The train left within a very few minutes, at eight-fifty. I hurried; the next one would leave at nine-thirty. There was hardly a soul on the platform. I went through the coaches; I remember a few farmers, a woman dressed in mourning, a young boy who was reading with fervor the *Annals* of Tacitus, a wounded and happy soldier. The coaches jerked forward at last. A man whom I recognized ran in vain to the end of the platform. It was Captain Richard Madden. Shattered, trembling, I shrank into the far corner of the seat, away from the dreaded window.

From this broken state I passed into an almost abject felicity. I told myself that the duel had already begun and that I had won the first encounter by frustrating, even if for forty minutes, even if by a stroke of fate, the attack of my adversary. I argued that this slightest of victories foreshadowed a total victory. I argued (no less fallaciously) that my cowardly felicity proved that I was a man capable of carrying out the adventure successfully. From this weakness I took strength that did not abandon me. I foresee that man will resign himself each day to more atrocious undertakings; soon there will be no one but warriors and brigands; I give them this counsel: *The author of an atrocious undertaking ought to imagine that he has already accomplished it, ought to impose upon himself a future as irrevocable as the past.* Thus I proceeded as my eyes of a man already dead registered the elapsing of that day, which was perhaps the last, and the diffusion of the night. The train ran gently along, amid ash trees. It stopped, almost in the middle of the fields. No one announced the name of the station. "Ashgrove?" I asked a few lads on the platform. "Ashgrove," they replied. I got off.

A lamp enlightened the platform but the faces of the boys were in shadow. One questioned me, "Are you going to Dr. Stephen Albert's house?" Without waiting for my answer, another said, "The house is a long way from here, but you won't get lost if you take this road to the left and at every crossroads turn again to your left." I tossed them a coin (my last), descended a few stone steps

and started down the solitary road. It went downhill, slowly. It was of elemental earth; overhead the branches were tangled; the low, full moon seemed to accompany me.

For an instant, I thought that Richard Madden in some way had penetrated my desperate plan. Very quickly, I understood that that was impossible. The instructions to turn always to the left reminded me that such was the common procedure for discovering the central point of certain labyrinths. I have some understanding of labyrinths: not for nothing am I the great-grandson of that Ts'ui Pên who was governor of Yunnan and who renounced worldly power in order to write a novel that might be even more populous than the *Hung Lu Meng* and to construct a labyrinth in which all men would become lost. Thirteen years he dedicated to these heterogeneous tasks, but the hand of a stranger murdered him—and his novel was incoherent and no one found the labyrinth. Beneath English trees I meditated on that lost maze: I imagined it inviolate and perfect at the secret crest of a mountain; I imagined it erased by rice fields or beneath the water; I imagined it infinite, no longer composed of octagonal kiosks and returning paths, but of rivers and provinces and kingdoms . . . I thought of a labyrinth of labyrinths, of one sinuous spreading labyrinth that would encompass the past and the future and in some way involve the stars. Absorbed in these illusory images, I forget my destiny of one pursued. I felt myself to be, for an unknown period of time, an abstract perceiver of the world. The vague, living countryside, the moon, the remains of the day worked on me, as well as the slope of the road which eliminated any possibility of weariness. The afternoon was intimate, infinite. The road descended and forked among the now confused meadows. A high-pitched, almost syllabic music approached and receded in the shifting of the wind, dimmed by leaves and distance. I thought that a man can be an enemy of other men, of the moments of other men, but not of a country: not of fireflies, words, gardens, streams of water, sunsets. Thus I arrived before a tall, rusty gate. Between the iron bars I made out a poplar grove and a pavilion. I understood suddenly two things, the first trivial, the second almost unbelievable: the music came from the pavilion, and the music was Chinese. For precisely that reason I had openly accepted it without paying it any heed. I do not remember whether there was a bell or whether I knocked with my hand. The sparkling of the music continued.

From the rear of the house within a lantern approached: a

lantern that the trees sometimes striped and sometimes eclipsed, a paper lantern that had the form of a drum and the color of the moon. A tall man bore it. I didn't see his face for the light blinded me. He opened the door and said slowly, in my own language: "I see that the pious Hsi P'êng persists in correcting my solitude. You no doubt wish to see the garden?"

I recognized the name of one of our consuls and I replied, disconcerted, "The garden?"

"The garden of forking paths."

Something stirred in my memory and I uttered with incomprehensible certainty, "The garden of my ancestor Ts'ui Pên."

"Your ancestor? Your illustrious ancestor? Come in."

The damp path zigzagged like those of my childhood. We came to a library of Eastern and Western books. I recognized bound in yellow silk several volumes of the Lost Encyclopedia, edited by the Third Emperor of the Luminous Dynasty but never printed. The record on the phonograph revolved next to a bronze phoenix. I also recall a *famille rose* vase and another, many centuries older, of that shade of blue which our craftsmen copied from the potter of Persia . . .

Stephen Albert observed me with a smile. He was, as I have said, very tall, sharp-featured, with gray eyes and a gray beard. He told me that he had been a missionary in Tientsin "before aspiring to become a Sinologist."

We sat down—I on a long, low divan, he with his back to the window and a tall circular clock. I calculated that my pursuer, Richard Madden, could not arrive for at least an hour. My irrevocable determination could wait.

"An astounding fate, that of Ts'ui Pên," Stephen Albert said. "Governor of his native province, learned in astronomy, in astrology and in the tireless interpretation of the canonical books, chess player, famous poet and calligrapher—he abandoned all this in order to compose a book and a maze. He renounced the pleasures of both tyranny and justice, of his populous couch, of his banquets and even of erudition—all to close himself up for thirteen years in the Pavilion of the Limpid Solitude. When he died, his heirs found nothing save chaotic manuscripts. His family, as you may be aware, wished to condemn them to the fire; but his executor—a Taoist or Buddhist monk—insisted on their publication."

"We descendants of Ts'ui Pên," I replied, "continue to curse that monk. Their publication was senseless. The book is an

indeterminate heap of contradictory drafts. I examined it once: in the third chapter the hero dies, in the fourth he is alive. As for the other undertaking of Ts'ui Pên, his labyrinth . . ."

"Here is Ts'ui Pên's labyrinth," he said, indicating a tall lacquered desk.

"An ivory labyrinth!" I exclaimed. "A minimum labyrinth."

"A labyrinth of symbols," he corrected. "An invisible labyrinth of time. To me, a barbarous Englishman, has been entrusted the revelation of this diaphanous mystery. After more than a hundred years, the details are irretrievable; but it is not hard to conjecture what happened. Ts'ui Pên must have said once: *I am withdrawing to write a book.* And another time: *I am withdrawing to construct a labyrinth.* Everyone imagined two works; to no one did it occur that the book and the maze were one and the same thing. The Pavilion of the Limpid Solitude stood in the center of a garden that was perhaps intricate; that circumstance could have suggested to the heirs a physical labyrinth. Hs'ui Pên died; no one in the vast territories that were his came upon the labyrinth; the confusion of the novel suggested to me that *it* was the maze. Two circumstances gave me the correct solution of the problem. One: the curious legend that Ts'ui Pên had planned to create a labyrinth which would be strictly infinite. The other: a fragment of a letter I discovered."

Albert rose. He turned his back on me for a moment; he opened a drawer of the black and gold desk. He faced me and in his hands he held a sheet of paper that had once been crimson, but was now pink and tenuous and cross-sectioned. The fame of Ts'ui Pên as a calligrapher had been justly won. I read, uncomprehendingly and with fervor, these words written with a minute brush by a man of my blood: *I leave to the various futures (not to all) my garden of forking paths.* Wordlessly, I returned the sheet. Albert continued:

"Before unearthing this letter, I had questioned myself about the ways in which a book can be infinite. I could think of nothing other than a cyclic volume, a circular one. A book whose last page was identical with the first, a book which had the possibility of continuing indefinitely. I remembered too that night which is at the middle of the Thousand and One Nights when Scheherazade (through a magical oversight of the copyist) begins to relate word for word the story of the Thousand and One Nights, establishing the risk of coming once again to the night when she must repeat it, and thus on to infinity. I imagined as

well a Platonic, hereditary work, transmitted from father to son, in which each new individual adds a chapter or corrects with pious care the pages of his elders. These conjectures diverted me; but none seemed to correspond, not even remotely, to the contradictory chapters of Ts'ui Pên. In the midst of this perplexity, I received from Oxford the manuscript you have examined. I lingered, naturally, on the sentence: *I leave to the various futures (not to all) my garden of forking paths.* Almost instantly, I understood: 'the garden of forking paths' was the chaotic novel; the phrase 'the various futures (not to all)' suggested to me the forking in time, not in space. A broad rereading of the work confirmed the theory. In all fictional works, each time a man is confronted with several alternatives, he chooses one and eliminates the others; in the fiction of Ts'ui Pên, he chooses—simultaneously—all of them. *He creates*, in this way, diverse futures, diverse times, which themselves also proliferate and fork. Here, then, is the explanation of the novel's contradictions. Fang, let us say, has a secret; a stranger calls at his door; Fang resolves to kill him. Naturally, there are several possible outcomes: Fang can kill the intruder, the intruder can kill Fang, they both can escape, they both can die, and so forth. In the work of Ts'ui Pên, all possible outcomes occur; each one is the point of departure for other forkings. Sometimes, the paths of this labyrinth converge: for example, you arrive at this house, but in one of the possible pasts you are my enemy, in another, my friend. If you will resign yourself to my incurable pronunciation, we shall read a few pages."

His face, within the vivid circle of the lamplight, was unquestionably that of an old man, but with something unalterable about it, even immortal. He read with slow precision two versions of the same epic chapter. In the first, an army marches to a battle across a lonely mountain; the horror of the rocks and shadows makes the men undervalue their lives and they gain an easy victory. In the second, the same army traverses a palace where a great festival is taking place; the resplendent battle seems to them a continuation of the celebration and they win the victory. I listened with proper veneration to these ancient narratives, perhaps less admirable in themselves than the fact that they had been created by my blood and were being restored to me by man of a remote empire, in the course of a desperate adventure, on a Western isle. I remember the last words, repeated in each version like a secret commandment: *Thus fought*

the heros, tranquil their admirable hearts, violent their swords, resigned to kill and to die.

From that moment on, I felt about me and within my dark body an invisible, intangible swarming. Not the swarming of the divergent, parallel, and finally coalescent armies, but a more inaccessible, more intimate agitation that they in some manner prefigured. Stephen Albert continued:

"I don't believe that your illustrious ancestor played idly with these variations. I don't consider it credible that he would sacrifice thirteen years to the infinite execution of a rhetorical experiment. In your country, the novel is a subsidiary form of literature; in Ts'ui Pên's time it was a despicable form. Ts'ui Pên was a brilliant novelist, but he was also a man of letters who doubtless did not consider himself a mere novelist. The testimony of his contemporaries proclaims— and his life fully confirms—his metaphysical and mystical interests. Philosophic controversy usurps a good part of the novel. I know that of all problems, none disturbed him so greatly nor worked upon him so much as the abysmal problem of time. Now then, the latter is the only problem that does not figure in the pages of the *Garden*. He does not even use the word that signifies *time*. How do you explain this voluntary omission?"

I proposed several solutions—all unsatisfactory. We discussed them. Finally, Stephen Albert said to me:

"In a riddle whose answer is chess, what is the only prohibited word?"

I thought a moment and replied, "The word *chess*."

"Precisely," said Albert. *"The Garden of Forking Paths* is an enormous riddle, or parable, whose theme is time; this recondite cause prohibits its mention. To omit a word always, to resort to inept metaphors and obvious periphrases, is perhaps the most emphatic way of stressing it. That is the tortuous method preferred, in each of the meanderings of his indefatigable novel, by the oblique Ts'ui Pên. I have compared hundreds of manuscripts, I have corrected the errors that the negligence of the copyists has introduced. I have guessed the plan of this chaos, I have re-established—I believe I have re-established—the primordial organization, I have translated the entire work: it is clear to me that not once does he employ the word 'time.' The explanation is obvious: *The Garden of Forking Paths* is an incomplete, but not false, image of the universe as Ts'ui Pên conceived it. In contrast to Newton and Schopenhauer, your ancestor did not

believe in a uniform, absolute time. He believed in an infinite series of times, in a growing, dizzying net of divergent, convergent and parallel times. This network of times which approached one another, forked, broke off, or were unaware of one another for centuries, embraces *all* possibilities of time. We do not exist in the majority of these times; in some you exist, and not I; in others I, and not you; in others, both of us. In the present one, which a favorable fate has granted me, you have arrived at my house; in another, while crossing the garden, you found me dead; in still another, I utter these same words, but I am a mistake, a ghost."

"In every one," I pronounced, not without a tremble to my voice, "I am grateful to you and revere you for your re-creation of the garden of Ts'ui Pên."

"Not in all," he murmured with a smile. "Time forks perpetually toward innumerable futures. In one of them I am your enemy."

Once again I felt the swarming sensation of which I have spoken. It seemed to me that the humid garden that surrounded the house was infinitely saturated with invisible persons. Those persons were Albert and I, secret, busy and multiform in other dimensions of time. I raised my eyes and the tenuous nightmare dissolved. In the yellow and black garden there was only one man; but this man was as strong as a statue . . . this man was approaching along the path and he was Captain Richard Madden.

"The future already exists," I replied, "but I am your friend. Could I see the letter again?"

Albert rose. Standing tall, he opened the drawer of the tall desk; for the moment his back was to me. I had readied the revolver. I fired with extreme caution. Albert fell uncomplainingly, immediately. I swear his death was instantaneous—a lightning stroke.

The rest is unreal, insignificant. Madden broke in, arrested me. I have been condemned to the gallows. I have won out abominably; I have communicated to Berlin the secret name of the city they must attack. They bombed it yesterday; I read it in the same papers that offered to England the mystery of the learned Sinologist Stephen Albert who was murdered by a stranger, one Yu Tsun. The Chief had deciphered this mystery. He knew my problem was to indicate (through the uproar of the war) the city called Albert, and that I had found no other means to do so than to kill a man of that name. He does not know (no one can know) my innumerable contrition and weariness.

Sunday Lemons

Derek Walcott

Desolate lemons, hold
tight, in your bowl of earth,
the light to your bitter flesh,

let a lemon glare
be all your armor
this naked Sunday,

your inflexible light
bounce off the shields of apples
so real, they seem waxen,

share your acid silence
with this woman's remembering
Sundays of other fruit,

till by concentration
you grow, a phalanx of helmets
braced for anything,

hexagonal cities were bees
died purely for sweetness,
your lamps be the last to go

on this polished table
this Sunday, which demands
more than the faith of candles

than helmeted conquistadors
dying like bees, multiplying
memories in her golden head;

as the afternoon vagues
into indigo, let your lamps
hold in this darkening earth

bowl, still life, but a life
beyond tears or the gaieties
of dew, the gay, neon damp

of the evening that blurs
the form of this woman lying,
a lemon, a flameless lamp.

What I Have Been Doing Lately

Jamaica Kincaid

WHAT I have been doing lately: I was lying in bed and the doorbell rang. I ran downstairs. Quick. I opened the door. There was no one there. I stepped outside. Either it was drizzling or there was a lot of dust in the air and the dust was damp. I stuck out my tongue and the drizzle or the damp dust tasted like government school ink. I looked north. I looked south. I decided to start walking north. While walking north, I noticed that I was barefoot. While walking north, I looked up and saw the planet Venus. I said, "It must be almost morning." I saw a monkey in a tree. The tree had no leaves. I said, "Ah, a monkey. Just look at that. A monkey." I walked for I don't know how long before I came up to a big body of water. I wanted to get across it but I couldn't swim. I wanted to get across it but would take me years to build a boat. I wanted to get across it but it would take me I didn't know how long to build a bridge. Years passed and then one day, feeling like it, I got into my boat and rowed across. When I got to the other side, it was noon and my shadow was small and fell beneath me. I set out on a path that stretched out straight ahead. I passed a house, and a dog was sitting on the verandah, but it looked the other way when it saw me coming. I passed a boy tossing a ball in the air but the boy looked the other way when he saw me coming. I walked and I walked but I couldn't tell if I walked a long time because my feet didn't feel as if they would drop off. I turned around to see what I had left behind me but nothing was familiar. Instead of the straight path, I saw hills. Instead of the boy with his ball, I saw tall flowering trees. I looked up and the sky was without clouds and seemed near, as if it were the ceiling in my house and, if I stood on a chair, I could touch it with the tips of my fingers. I turned around and looked ahead of me again. A deep hole had opened up before me. I looked in. The hole was deep and dark and I couldn't see the bottom. I thought, What's down there? so on purpose I fell in. I fell and I fell, over and over, as if I were an old suitcase. On the sides of the deep hole I could see things written,

but perhaps it was in a foreign language because I couldn't read them. Still I fell, for I don't know how long. As I fell I began to see that I didn't like the way falling made me feel. Falling made me feel sick and I missed all the people I had loved. I said, "I don't want to fall anymore," and I reversed myself. I was standing again on the edge of the deep hole. I looked at the deep hole and I said, "You can close up now," and it did. I walked some more without knowing distance. I only knew that I passed through days and nights, I only knew that I passed through rain and shine, light and darkness. I was never thirsty and I felt no pain. Looking at the horizon, I made a joke for myself: I said, "The earth has thin lips," and I laughed.

Looking at the horizon again, I saw a lone figure coming toward me, but I wasn't frightened because I was sure it was my mother. As I got closer to the figure, I could see that it wasn't my mother, but I still wasn't frightened because I could see that it was a woman.

When this woman got closer to me, she looked at me hard and then she threw up her hands. She must have seen me somewhere before because she said, "It's you. Just look at that. It's you. And just what have you been doing lately?"

I could have said, "I have been praying not to grow any taller."

I could have said, "I have been listening carefully to my mother's words, so as to make a good imitation of a dutiful daughter."

I could have said, "A pack of dogs, tired from chasing each other all over town, slept in the moonlight."

Instead, I said, "What I have been doing lately: I was lying in bed on my back, my hands drawn up, my fingers interlaced lightly at the nape of my neck. Someone rang the doorbell. I went downstairs and opened the door but there was no one there. I stepped outside. Either it was drizzling or there was a lot of dust in the air and the dust was damp. I stuck out my tongue and the drizzle or the damp dust tasked like government school ink. I looked north and I looked south. I started walking north. While walking north, I wanted to move fast, so I removed the shoes from my feet. While walking north, I looked up and saw the planet Venus, and I said, 'If the sun went out, it would be eight minutes before I would know it.' I saw a monkey sitting in a tree that had no leaves and I said, 'A monkey. Just look at that. A monkey. I picked up a stone and I threw it at the monkey.' The monkey, seeing the stone, quickly moved out of its way. Three times I threw a stone at the monkey and three times it moved

away. The fourth time I threw the stone, the monkey caught it and threw it back at me. The stone struck me on my forehead over my right eye, making a deep gash. The gash healed immediately but now the skin on my forehead felt false to me. I walked for I don't know how long before I came to a big body of water. I wanted to get across, so when the boat came I paid my fare. When I got to the other side, I saw a lot of people sitting on the beach and they were having a picnic. They were the most beautiful people I had ever seen. Everything about them was black and shiny. Their skin was black and shiny. Their shoes were black and shiny. Their hair was black and shiny. The clothes they wore were black and shiny. I could hear them laughing and chatting and I said, 'I would like to be with these people,' so I started to walk toward them; but when I got up close to them I saw that they weren't at a picnic and they weren't beautiful and they weren't chatting and laughing. All around me was black mud and the people all looked as if they had been made up out of the black mud. I looked up and saw that the sky seemed far away and nothing I could stand on would make me able to touch it with my fingertips. I thought, If only I could get out of this, so I started to walk. I must have walked for a long time because my feet hurt and felt as if they would drop off. I thought, If only just around the bend I would see my house and inside my house I would find my bed, freshly made at that, and in the kitchen I would find my mother or anyone else that I loved making me a custard. I thought, If only it was a Sunday and I was sitting in a church and I had just heard someone sing a psalm. I felt very sad so I sat down. I felt so sad that I rested my head on my own knees and smoothed my own head. I felt so sad I couldn't imagine feeling any other way again. I said, 'I don't like this. I don't want to do this anymore.' And I went back to lying in bed, just before the doorbell rang."

Biographical Notes

Italo Calvino (1923–1985) Italo Calvino (ē tal´ ō kal vē´ nō) grew up on the Italian Riviera at San Remo. During World War II, he fought against Fascist control of Italy and the Nazi occupation. Following the war, he emerged as one of Italy's most inventive writers, whose work has been internationally praised for its imagination, humor, and mixture of actual and fanciful elements.

Wislawa Szymborska (born 1923) Winner of the Nobel Prize for Literature, Wislawa Szymborska (vē swä´ vä shim bô r´ skä) has won international acclaim as a poet and commands great popularity with the general reading public. For example, in her native Poland, one of her books of poems, *A Great Number*, sold 10,000 copies in only one week!

Elie Wiesel (born 1928) Elie Wiesel (el´ ē vē zel´) grew up in the Carpathian Mountains in the village of Sighet. When Nazis arrived and rounded up all the Jews, Wiesel and his family were sent to the Auschwitz concentration camp. His mother and younger sister were gassed to death, and Elie and his father were sent to Buchenwald, another camp, where they were treated cruelly. Elie's father died there of starvation and disease. Ten years after being liberated from Buchenwald, Wiesel wrote *Night*, in which he recounts for the world the horrors and atrocities of the Holocaust.

James Joyce (1882–1941) All of James Joyce's works are set in his native Dublin, and all have firm roots in literary traditions of the past. Joyce's ability, however, to reinterpret and transform these familiar literary forms are the hallmarks of his greatness as a writer.

Rainer Maria Rilke (1875–1926) Born in Prague to German-speaking parents, Rainer Maria Rilke (rī´ nər mä rē´ ä ril´ kə) had a miserable childhood and throughout much of his life preferred solitude. Following college, Rilke defied his parents, who wanted him to pursue a career in business or law, and instead focused his effort on writing poetry. He is now recognized as one of the finest poets ever to write in the German language.

Stanislaw Lem (born 1921) A study in contradiction, Stanislaw Lem (stan´ is läf lem) is an acknowledged expert in cybernetics,

the study of human and machine intelligence, yet he cannot work his son's computer and prefers to turn out his manuscripts by hand. Lem turned to writing science fiction because he believes it allows him to convey the uncertainty that his war-torn childhood ingrained in him.

Primo Levi (1919–1987) Primo Levi (prē´ mō lā´ vē) was probably best known as a survivor and chronicler of the Nazi Holocaust. However, in his short stories, novels, poetry, and essays, Levi allowed his formidable curiosity to wander widely, writing about nature, science, and his own life. In the process, he came to be regarded as one of the twentieth century's most important and least classifiable writers.

Anna Akhmatova (1889–1966) Anna Akhmatova (uk mät´ ə və) was born in a small town on the coast of the Black Sea near Odessa. She changed her name at the request of her father, who shunned her and her career as a poet. During Joseph Stalin's purge of writers and intellectuals in the late 1930's, her poetry was banned and her life threatened. However, Akhmatova persisted, and when the ban was lifted, she published several more volumes of highly regarded poetry.

Albert Camus (1913–1960) French author Albert Camus (al bär´ kȧ mü) was born and raised in Algeria, a colony of France, to parents of European descent. Personally affected by war and tragedy, Camus focused on the human experience and condition in his literary works. He was awarded the Nobel Prize for Literature in 1957.

Federico García Lorca (1898–1936) Federico García Lorca, (fe´de rē´ kô gär sē´ ä lô r´ kä) considered by many to be Spain's most accomplished poet and playwright, derived inspiration from the people and culture of his homeland, Andalusia, near Granada. Although García Lorca did not intend for his poems to be political, the Spanish government and those in the rising Nationalist Movement disagreed. He was assassinated in 1936 in an effort by the government to purge all "undesirables."

Isak Dinesen (1885–1962) Isak Dinesen was born in Denmark and moved to British East Africa (now Kenya) in 1914 following her marriage. Although her marriage failed, Dinesen stayed in Africa until 1931, when falling coffee prices forced her to abandon

her coffee plantation. Dinesen's remarkable life was captured in the Academy Award-winning movie *Out of Africa*, which was based on her autobiographical novel.

Yukio Mishima (1925–1970) Writer Yukio Mishima (yōo´ kē ō´ mish´ i mä´) explored cultural dislocation in postwar Japan in his writings. He is perhaps best known for his novel *Rashomon*. In 1970, Mishima publically committed hari-kari to protest the Westernization of Japan.

Aisin-Gioro P'u Yi (1906–1967) The last emperor of China, Aisin-Gioro P'u Yi (ā Hin jüe lō pōo yē) was forced to abdicate at age twelve but was allowed to retain many privileges. In 1924, P'u Yi was forced to leave the Imperial Palace and for a time took refuge outside of China. His autobiography was published in 1960.

Akutagawa Ryunosuke (1892–1927) Best known for his short stories, Akutagawa Ryunosuke (ä kōo tä gä wä ryōo nō sōo ke) also wrote poems and essays. He became an instant literary figure following publication of "The Nose." Most of Ryunosuke's stories are characterized by strange and unsettling occurrences, which perhaps reveal his ultimate disaffection for the world around him.

Santha Rama Rau (born 1923) The daughter of world travelers, Santha Rama Rau (sän´ thä räm´ ä rou) grew up with more freedoms than most young girls her age. Her father was an Indian diplomat while India was still a colony of Britain. After having spent a good deal of her teenage years in London, Rama Rau returned to India and found herself a stranger in her own land. She addressed the subject of her heritage and identity in several works, such as *Home to India*, written when she was a student at Wellesley College.

Mark Mathabane (born 1960) Mark Mathabane (mä tä bä´ne) grew up in Alexandra, a poor black town just outside Johannesburg, South Africa. Because of apartheid—racial discriminatory laws—he was required to attend an all-black school for which his family had to pay tuition. *Kaffir Boy*, Mathabane's autobiographical account of growing up black under apartheid, was banned in his homeland. It has, however, become a worldwide bestseller.

Chinua Achebe (born 1930) Chinua Achebe was born in Nigeria to an Ibo father who had converted to Christianity and as a result, learned firsthand about the differences between cultures. This understanding informs much of his writing. His novel *Things Fall Apart* is highly regarded by critics and the reading public alike.

Wole Soyinka (born 1934) Born in western Nigeria, Wole Soyinka (wō´ lā shō yin´ kə) was raised Christian yet was influenced by the Yoruba, with their rich cultural traditions. Politically active, Soyinka has used his poetry, plays, and other writings to get his political messages across. At one point, his political writings landed him in jail, although that did not deter him from writing secretly in his jail cell. In 1986, Soyinka was awarded the Nobel Prize for Literature, becoming the first black African ever to be so recognized.

Doris Lessing (born 1919) Doris Lessing is sometimes considered a British writer, although she was born in Persia and raised in the British colony of Rhodesia (now the independent country of Zimbabwe) in south-central Africa. Among her best-known works is the novel *The Grass Is Singing*, in which Lessing explores the injustices suffered by Africans at the hands of European colonists.

Yehuda Amichai (born 1924) Yehuda Amichai (ye hoo´ də ä´ mi̱ khī) was born in Germany, the son of Orthodox Jews. Fortunately, before the outbreak of World War II, Amichai and his family relocated to Palestine—the region that became Israel in 1948. In addition to being a writer, Amichai is a man of action. He served with England's Jewish Brigade in Egypt in World War II, and after the war, he was a soldier with the Israeli defense forces for Israel's War of Independence.

Naguib Mahfouz (born 1911) Naguib Mahfouz (nä´ hēb´ mä´ fōoz) has long been considered by the Arab world to be its greatest living novelist, but winning the Nobel Prize for Literature in 1988 brought him international recognition. The old quarter of Cairo, in which he was born, is the setting for many of his works. Now almost deaf and partially blind, Mahfouz claims to live only to write. He has said: "If the urge should ever leave me, I want that day to be my last."

Biographical Notes

Julio Cortázar (1914–1984) Fiction writer Julio Cortázar (hoō lē ō kôr tä´ zər) was born in Brussels, Belgium, of Argentinian parents, and although he returned to Argentina when still young, he seemed to have a sense of belonging to both South America and Europe. Cortázar's fiction became famous for its off-beat sense of fun and fantasy. For example, *Hopscotch* contains instructions for reading the story in at least two different ways.

Gabriela Mistral (1889–1957) At fifteen years of age, without having finished school herself, Gabriela Mistral (gà brē e´ là mē sträl´) began teaching school in a small village near Montegrande, Chile, her childhood home. When she turned to writing poems, Mistral wrote most often about women's and children's issues, which were dear to her heart. When she heard the news about being awarded the Nobel Prize in 1945, Mistral declared, "Perhaps it was because I was the candidate of the women and children."

Octavio Paz (born 1914) Octavio Paz (ôk tä´ vyô päs) was born in a suburb of Mexico City and at a very young age discovered an interest in poetry. Soon after graduating from college, *Forest Moon*, his first volume of poetry, was published, and he soon gained literary fame. Following Latin American tradition, Paz, as a literary celebrity, was appointed to several diplomatic posts and traveled the world. No matter how far his travels take him, Paz has never given up his Mexican identity nor forgotten his Mexican heritage. In 1990, Paz was awarded the Nobel Prize for Literature.

Jorge Luis Borges (1899–1986) Born to a wealthy Buenos Aires family, Jorge Luis Borges (hôr´ he loō ēs´ bôr´ hes) had a paternal grandfather who was English. From an early age, he was able to read and speak both English and Spanish. After World War II, Borges founded his own group of young writers and contributed fiction to Argentine literary magazines. In 1961, he shared the International Publisher's Prize with Irish author Samuel Beckett.

Derek Walcott (born 1930) Famed poet and playwright Derek Walcott was born on St. Lucia, a West Indian island. His racial and ethnic background is mixed, and he grew up speaking both the dialect of the island and English. His inventive and fresh use of the English language is groundbreaking.

Jamaica Kincaid (born 1949) Now a resident of Vermont, Jamaica Kincaid was born on the tiny Caribbean island of Antigua. Raised in St. John's, Antigua's largest city, Kincaid came to hate the European colonialism that had exploited her people for many centuries. Kincaid attended college in New Hampshire and afterward found work writing for a teenage girls' magazine. She eventually published her first story in *The New Yorker* and has found success as a writer ever since.

Acknowledgments

Pantheon Books, an imprint of Random House, Inc.
"Axolotl" by Julio Cortázar, from *End of the Game and Other Stories* by Julio Cortázar, translated by Paul Blackburn. Copyright © 1967 by Random House, Inc. Reprinted by permission of Pantheon Books, a division of Random House, Inc.

Random House, Inc., and The Rungstedlund Foundation of Denmark
Excerpt from *Out of Africa* by Isak Dinesen. Copyright 1937 by Random House, Inc., and renewed © 1965 by The Rungstedlund Foundation of Denmark. Reprinted by permission.

Regents of the University of California, the University of California Press, and Chana Bloch
"Seven Laments for the War-Dead," translated by Chana Bloch, from *The Selected Poetry of Yehuda Amichai*, translated and edited by Chana Bloch and Stephen Mitchell. Copyright © 1996 The Regents of the University of California. Permission granted by the Regents of the University of California and the University of California Press and the translator.

Simon & Schuster
Excerpt from *Kaffir Boy* by Mark Mathabane is reprinted with the permission of Simon & Schuster. Copyright © 1986 by Mark Mathabane.

Simon & Schuster and Jonathan Clowes Ltd.
"A Sunrise on the Veld" by Doris Lessing is reprinted with the permission of Simon & Schuster and Johnathan Clowes Ltd., London, on behalf of Doris Lessing, from *African Stories* and from *This Was the Old Chief's Country* (in England) by Doris Lessing. Copyright 1951 Doris Lessing. Copyright © 1981 by Doris Lessing.

Wole Soyinka
"Telephone Conversation" by Wole Soyinka from *Reflections: Nigerian Prose and Verse*, edited by Frances Ademola. Copyright © 1962 by African Universities Press Ltd., Lagos. Reprinted by permission of the author.

Viking Penguin, a division of Penguin Putnam Inc.
In the Land of Small Dragon: A Vietnamese Folktale by Dang Manh Kha, as told to Ann Nolan Clark. Copyright © 1979 Ann Nolan Clark. "Eveline" from *Dubliners* by James Joyce. Copyright 1916 by B. W. Beubsch. Definitive text Copyright © 1967 by the Estate of James Joyce. Used by permission of Viking Penguin, a division of Penguin Putnam Inc.

Zephyr Press
"Lot's Wife" by Anna Akhmatova, from *The Complete Poems of Anna Akhmatova*, translated by Judith Hemschemeyer, edited by Roberta Reeder. Translation copyright © 1983, 1984, 1985, 1986, 1987, 1988, 1989, 1992 by Judith Hemschemeyer. Reprinted by permission of Zephyr Press.

Note: Every effort has been made to locate the copyright owner of material reprinted in this book. Omissions brought to our attention will be corrected in subsequent editions.